Keyboard Instruction  with CD Included

MODERN JAZZ PIANO

An Intermediate Guide to Jazz Concepts, Improvisation, Technique, and Theory

By Sarah Jane Cion

ISBN 0-634-08366-X

7777 W. BLUEMOUND RD. P.O. BOX 13819 MILWAUKEE, WI 53213

In Australia Contact:
Hal Leonard Australia Pty. Ltd.
4 Lentara Court
Cheltenham, Victoria, 3192 Australia
Email: ausadmin@halleonard.com

Visit Hal Leonard Online at
www.halleonard.com

TABLE OF CONTENTS

INTRODUCTION

Jazz is a living, breathing thing—an entity—and a growing energy all its own. I'm excited to present the building blocks that provide the foundation for jazz improvisation. This book is geared toward the student who has already achieved an intermediate level of sight-reading and technical facility, but who has had limited exposure to jazz along the way.

I believe this book provides an entrée into the world of harmony, rhythm, and improvisation, which are essential to jazz but often overlooked by classical teachers in their efforts to teach the notes written on a page. I started to write this book because of all the students I've taught over the years. Time and time again, I see their faces light up as I explain the basic concepts of intervals, 7th chords, harmonic progressions, and the symmetrical nature of the 12-tone scale.

That process of discovery has continued to inspire me throughout the years. I continue to have the pleasure of watching my students discover the wonder and joys of hearing and playing jazz; this is what led me to put into book form some of the concepts that allowed me to make these wonderful discoveries myself. Each concept is offered here with an explanation, exercises, and practical tools for the student to work with. This book should supplement working with a jazz piano teacher, because nothing replaces the experience of listening, imitating, and receiving personal guidance on the path. And keep in mind that the most important thing to do as you learn to play jazz is to listen, listen, listen! Enjoy!

-Sarah Jane Cion, March 2004

DEDICATION

This book is dedicated to Charlie Banacos, a great teacher and mentor.

ACKNOWLEDGMENTS

Special thanks to Phil Palombi, Lara Palombi, Carol and Rich Palombi, Nicole Pasternack, Vince Scuderi, Maxyne Lang, all at Hal Leonard, Steve Getz, Jay Shornstein, Scott Latzky, Carolyn Steinberg, Jane Sweeney, Laura Dreyer, Peter Cassino, Andy LaVerne, Mike Longo, Fred Hersch, Audrey Welber, Derrick Boelter, Elizabeth Heller, Murray Cion, Jim Klein, and James McBride.

CYCLE OF 4THS

As jazz players, we practice things in all twelve keys, which enables us to transpose with ease. Taking the 4th note of every major scale beginning in the key of C cycles us through all twelve keys. The preferable order of keys to practice in is the cycle of 4ths: C, F, B♭, E♭, A♭, D♭, G♭ (or F♯), B, E, A, D, and G. See the chart below.

Cycle of 4ths

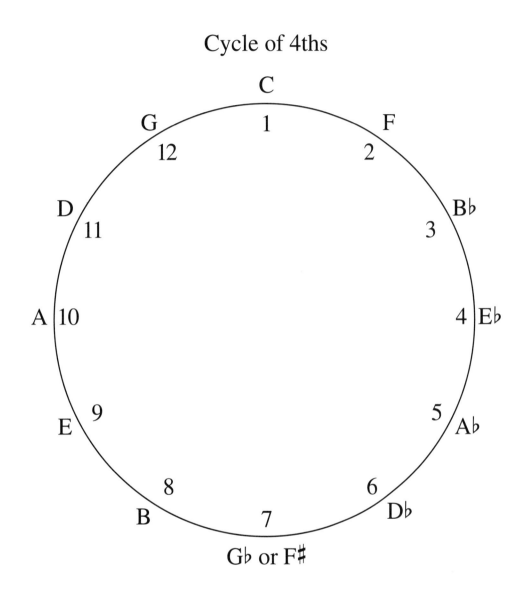

Enharmonically we generally gravitate towards keys with the least amount of accidentals. For example, the notes in a G♭ major 7th chord are G♭, B♭, D♭, and F (three accidentals). Its enharmonic F♯ major 7th is spelled F♯, A♯, C♯, and E♯ (four accidentals). Theoretically speaking, the notes in a G♭ minor 7th chord are G♭, B♭♭, D♭, and F♭ (four accidentals). However, the notes in an F♯ minor 7th chord are F♯, A, C♯, and E (two accidentals). Therefore we will use G♭ and F♯ interchangeably, according to each specific example.

KEY SCALES

A major scale consists of a series of seven tones (eight including the octave) built with whole steps and half steps. A half step is any two notes that are directly next to each other. A whole step is any two notes with a half step in between. The order of steps for any major scale is always the same: whole, whole, half, whole, whole, whole, half.

This is demonstrated below with a C major scale.

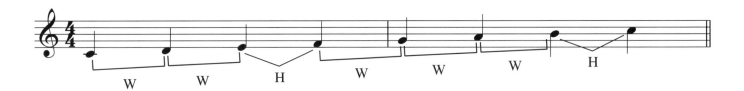

The *relative minor* scale shares the same key signature as its major counterpart. A relative minor key begins on the 6th tone of the major scale. For example, if we count through the notes of the above C major scale, we'll find that A is the 6th tone. Therefore, A minor is the relative minor of C major. Another way to identify the relative minor is to count down three half steps from the root of the major key: C to B, B to B♭, B♭ to A.

In the order of the cycle of 4ths, play each major scale up and down from octave to octave. Then play each relative minor scale, octave to octave.

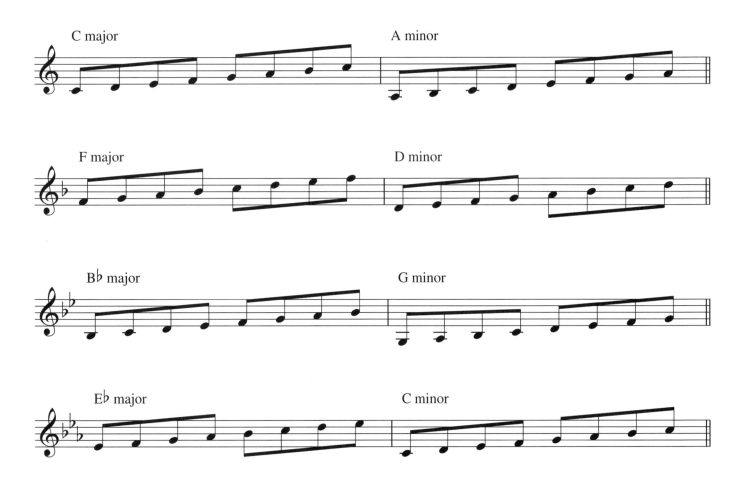

BASIC INTERVALS

An *interval* is defined as the distance between two notes. We already learned two intervals earlier: the half step and whole step. (These intervals also have other names, which we'll see in the following example.) Below are the twelve intervals (thirteen including the octave) that are created within a major scale. Play each interval below in two ways: melodically (two tones one after the other) and harmonically (two tones at the same time).

minor 2nd = half step

major 2nd = whole step

minor 3rd = whole step + half step

major 3rd = 2 whole steps

perfect 4th = major 3rd + half step

tritone or augmented 4th
(divides the octave exactly in half)

tritone = diminished or flatted fifth

perfect 5th

minor 6th

major 6th

minor 7th

major 7th

Octave

In jazz we count intervals at the very least up to the 13th, which is six notes above the octave. We especially need to be familiar with the 9th, 10th, 11th, and 13th, as these are the important tensions that we will use in the language of jazz harmony.

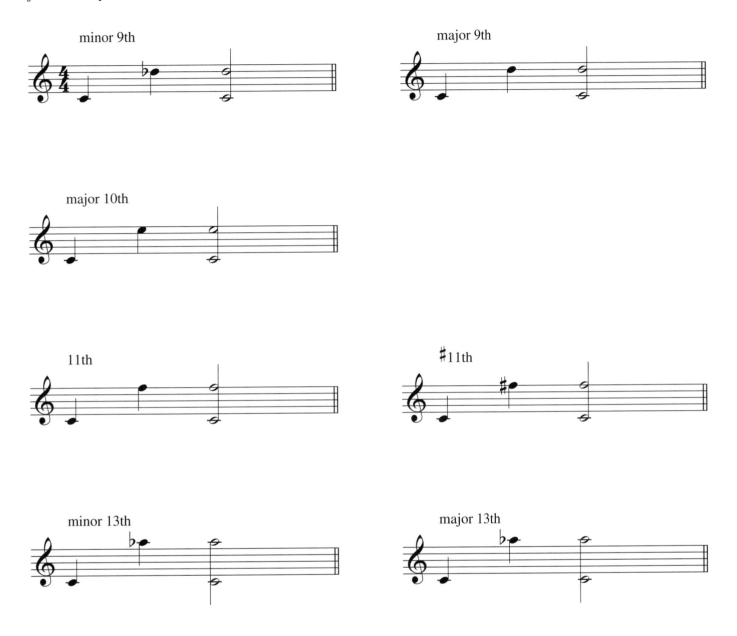

Practice playing random intervals beginning on any note and identify them by ear. Ear training is one of the most important aspects of playing improvised music.

Now let's identify the intervals found in the tune on the following page, "More than Every Star." There are two types of intervals to be identified: linear (melodic) and vertical (harmonic).

Play each melody note back to back and identify the distance between each note. This will be the melodic interval. For example, the first interval between melody notes G and D is a perfect 5th.

Next, identify the interval between the bass note indicated by the chord symbol and each melody note. This will be the harmonic interval. For example, the interval created between Cm7 in the bass and the G in the melody is also a perfect 5th.

Many of the intervals have been labeled in the intro and A section to start you out. See if you can figure out the B section on your own.

MORE THAN EVERY STAR

By SARAH JANE CION

TRIADS AND 7TH CHORDS

When you build a 3rd on each degree of the major scale, you create two qualities of intervals. These qualities are major and minor. The order of 3rds for any major scale is major, minor, minor, major, major, minor, minor. See below.

Triads

When you build a triad on each degree of the major scale you create three qualities of triads. These qualities are major, minor, and diminished. A triad consists of two thirds stacked on top of each other, from bottom to top. The order of triads for any major scale is major, minor, minor, major, major, minor, diminished. The interval structure for the these three triads is as follows:

- Major Triad = major 3rd on bottom, minor 3rd on top
- Minor Triad = minor 3rd on bottom, major 3rd on top
- Diminished Triad = minor 3rd on bottom, minor 3rd on top

Note: In chord symbols, the word "diminished" is often represented by the symbol °.

7th Chords

When you build a 7th chord on each degree of the major scale you create four qualities of chords. These qualities are major, minor, dominant, and half-diminished. (Another term for half-diminished is minor 7 flat 5.)
A 7th chord consists of a triad plus the interval of a 7th from the root. The order of 7th chords for a major scale is major, minor, minor, major, dominant, minor, and half-diminished. The interval structure for the these chords is as follows:

- Major 7th Chord = major triad + major 7th
- Minor 7th Chord = minor triad + minor 7th
- Dominant 7th Chord = major triad + minor 7th
- Half-Diminished Chord = diminished triad + minor 7th

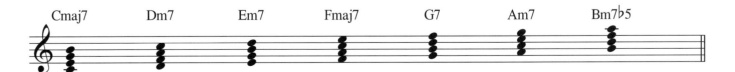

For the following exercises, build and play the structure indicated without reading the music. It's just provided for reference.

Build a major 3rd on every note in the cycle of 4ths. Name the interval aloud as you go.

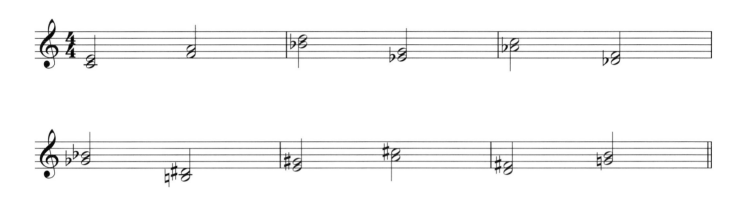

Build a minor 3rd on every note in the cycle of 4ths. Name the interval aloud as you go.

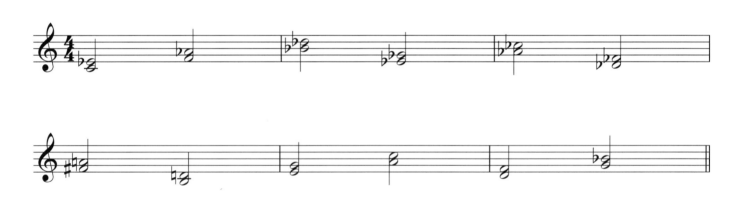

Build a major triad on every note in the cycle of 4ths. Say the name of the triad aloud beginning with the root, then name the quality.

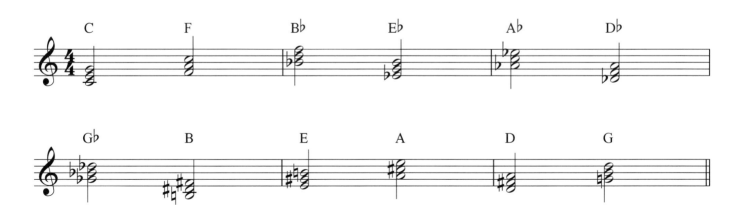

Build a minor triad on every note in the cycle of 4ths. Say the name of the triad aloud beginning with the root, then name the quality.

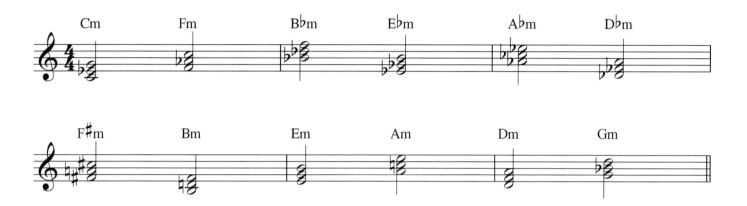

Build a diminished triad on every note in the cycle of 4ths. Say the name of the triad aloud beginning with the root, then name the quality.

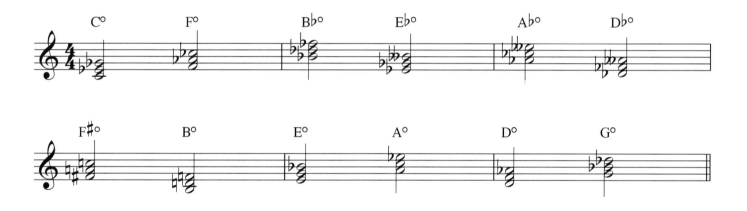

Build a major 7th chord on every note in the cycle of 4ths. Say the name of the chord aloud beginning with the root, then name the quality.

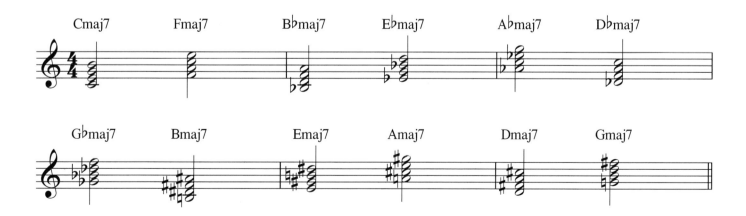

Build a dominant 7th chord on every note in the cycle of 4ths. To go from a major 7th to a dominant chord, simply lower the 7th one half step. Say the name of the chord aloud beginning with the root, then name the quality.

Build a minor 7th chord on every note in the cycle of 4ths. To go from a dominant 7th to a minor 7th chord, lower the 3rd one half step. Say the name of the chord aloud beginning with the root, then name the quality.

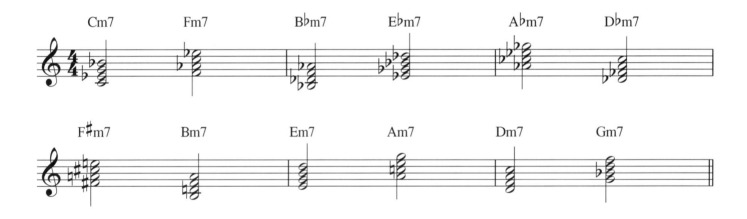

Build a half-diminished chord on every note in the cycle of 4ths. To go from a minor 7th to a half-diminished chord, lower the 5th one half step. Say the name of the chord aloud beginning with the root, then name the quality.

Chord Scales

Finding a scale that fits over a chord is vital to jazz improvisation. One way to do this is to find a note (or more than one note) that fits between each chord tone. We call this a passing tone.

For example, find a note that fits between the root and the 3rd and run the three notes up and down. Repeat this process for the 3rd and 5th, and for the 5th and 7th. This is demonstrated below with a Cmaj7 chord.

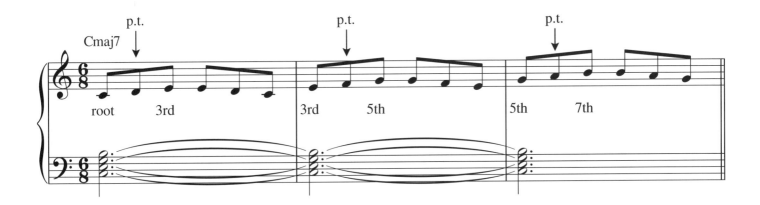

When you have identified three appropriate passing tones, run the resulting scale up and down a couple of times. In this case, we end up with a C major scale.

Sometimes there will be more than one passing tone that fits well between chord tones. In a minor 7th chord for instance, both a ♭6th and a ♮6th fit between the 5th and 7th.

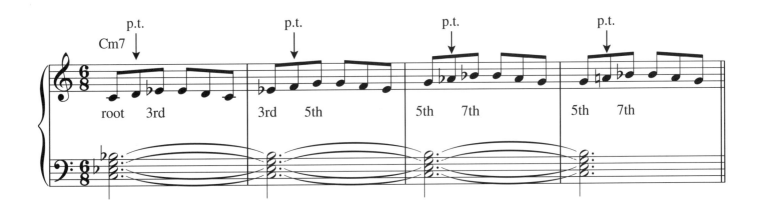

Practice both scales that are created—the first with a ♭6th, and the second with a ♮6th.

There are a few different passing tones that fit between the chord tones of a dominant 7th chord. The most basic choices create a simple major scale with a ♭7th.

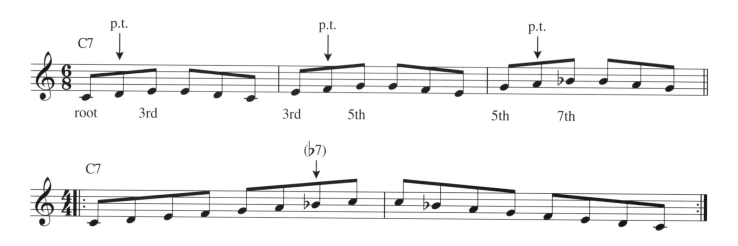

Sometimes if more than one passing tone fits between chord tones, you can play them in the same scale. In a dominant 7th chord, both a ♭9 and ♯9 fit between the root and the 3rd. Also notice the choice of a raised 4th (sharp 11th) between the 3rd and 5th chord tones.

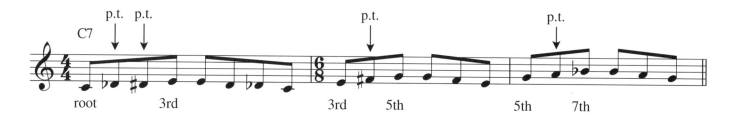

The scale that results from these choices is a half-whole diminished scale. For a detailed explanation of this wonderfully symmetric scale, see the section on diminished scales and chords.

Find chord scales for major, minor, and dominant 7th chords in every key in the cycle of 4ths.

INVERSIONS

An inversion is created when a note other than the root appears at the bottom of a chord. For example, when you take a root-position triad (one in which the root is the lowest note) and move the bottom note (the root) to the top, you create a *first-inversion* triad. A first-inversion triad has the 3rd of the chord on the bottom. When you move the bottom note of the first inversion triad (the 3rd) to the top, you create a second-inversion triad. A *second-inversion* triad has the 5th of the chord on the bottom.

Play each major triad and its inversions in every key in the cycle of 4ths. Name aloud the root of the chord, the quality, and the inversion.

root   1st   2nd   root
position inversion inversion position   (etc.)

Play each minor triad and its inversions in every key in the cycle of 4ths. Name aloud the root of the chord, the quality, and the inversion.

(etc.)

Play each diminished triad and its inversions in every key in the cycle of 4ths. Name aloud the root of the chord, the quality, and the inversion.

(etc.)

7th Chords

7th chords can be inverted just as triads can be. However, since there are four notes in the 7th chord, there is another possibility. Along with the first inversion (3rd on bottom) and second inversion (5th on bottom), a *third inversion* results from placing the 7th on bottom.

Play a major 7th chord and its inversions on every note in the cycle of 4ths. Say the name of the inversion aloud beginning with the root of the chord.

root 1st 2nd 3rd
position inversion inversion inversion

(etc.)

Play a dominant 7th chord and its inversions on every note in the cycle of 4ths. Say the name of the inversion aloud beginning with the root of the chord.

(etc.)

Play a minor 7th chord and its inversions on every note in the cycle of 4ths. Say the name of the inversion aloud beginning with the root of the chord.

(etc.)

Play a half-diminished 7th chord and its inversions on every note in the cycle of 4ths. Say the name of the inversion aloud beginning with the root of the chord.

(etc.)

Now let's utilize inversions in a practical application. Inversions make the movement between chords as effortless as possible. Ground your ear to the key by playing the root of the chord in the left hand.

A 7th chord in root position followed by a second-inversion 7th chord provides the best voice leading when cycling through 4ths. Practice alternating the two inversions throughout the cycle of 4ths.

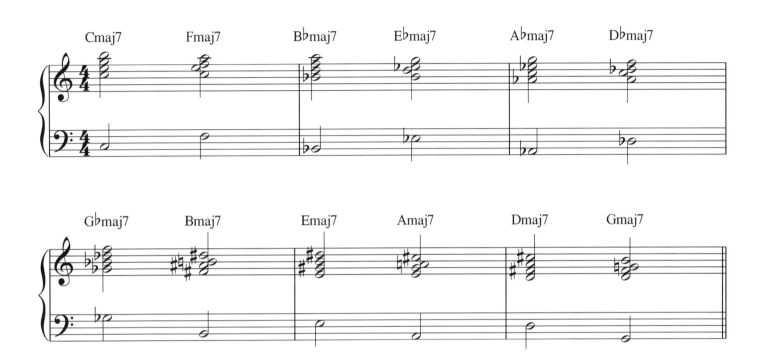

A 7th chord in first inversion followed by a third-inversion chord also provides good voice leading. Practice alternating these two inversions throughout the cycle of 4ths.

Now begin on a Cmaj7 chord in second inversion. A root-position 7th chord following this provides the best voice leading in the cycle of 4ths. Practice alternating these two inversions throughout the cycle of 4ths.

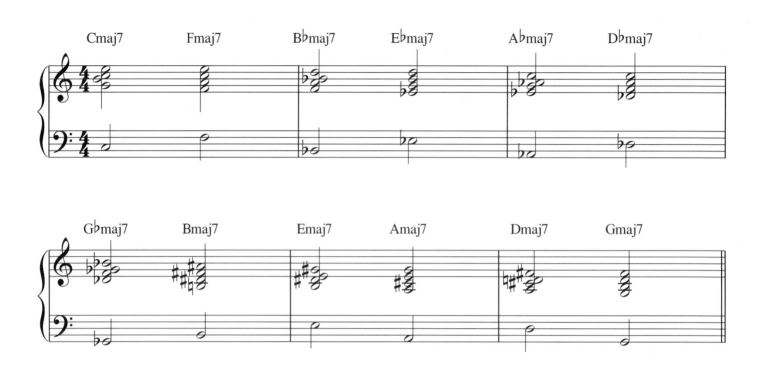

Finally, practice alternating between third-inversion and first-inversion 7th chords. This is the last of the four possible pairings.

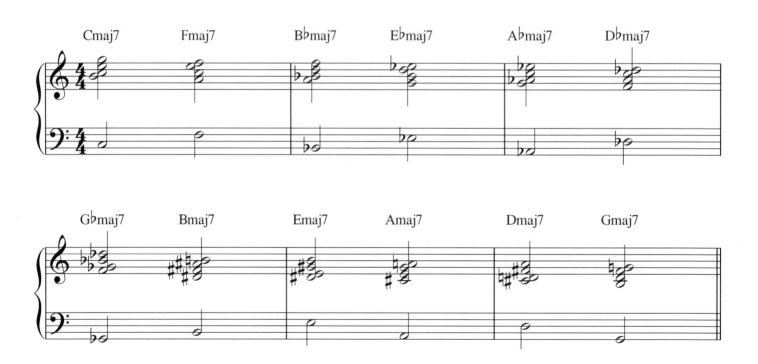

It is vital to practice these four pairs of inversions on dominant and minor 7th chords as well.

Now we will practice these four sets of inversion pairings in the left hand. Developing fluidity between 7th chords in the left hand:

- allows the right hand to improvise freely;
- provides a solid harmonic foundation;
- eliminates the need to jump from root position to root position as in the old style of ragtime.

When voicings get too low on the keyboard they begin to sound muddy. At these junctures it is important to adjust the range by transposing up an octave. Below we see the four possible inversion pairings through the cycle of 4ths as played by the left hand.

It is essential to practice these four pairs of inversions on dominant and minor 7th chords as well.

ARPEGGIATION

An *arpeggio* is simply the notes of a chord played separately, as a melody. Arpeggiation is one of the most important tools for improvisation. A great way to practice is to arpeggiate each 7th chord through all its inversions. Play the eighth notes as evenly as possible, as if you were playing a classical etude. The use of a metronome is extremely beneficial to establish good rhythmic habits.

Play a maj7 chord in the LH while arpeggiating a maj7 chord in the RH in root position. Then arpeggiate the first, second, and third inversions up and down the keyboard. Play this exercise in all twelve keys in the cycle of 4ths.

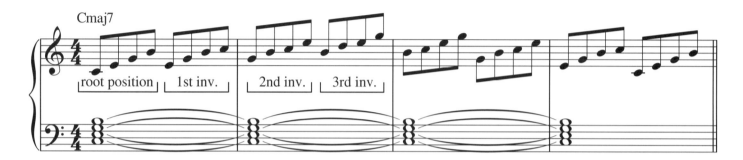

Now practice this exercise with dominant 7th chords in all keys through the cycle of 4ths.

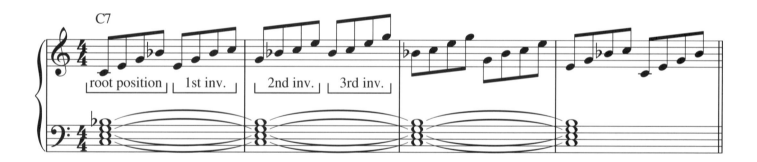

Now practice this exercise with minor 7th chords in all keys through the cycle of 4ths.

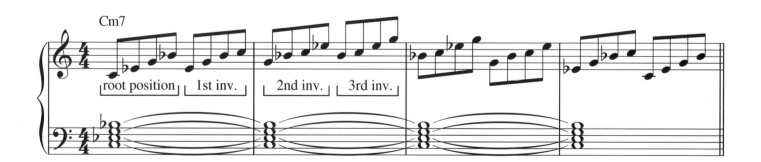

Repeat this exercise on the half-diminished chords using the same technique. Play this example in all twelve keys in the cycle of 4ths.

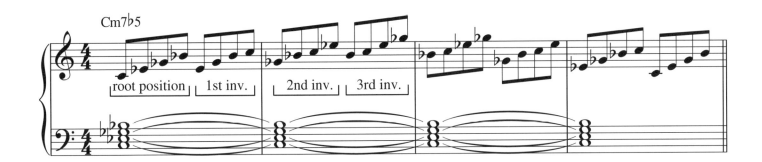

Finally, we have the fully-diminished 7th chords. Practice in all twelve keys, beginning on each note in the cycle of 4ths.

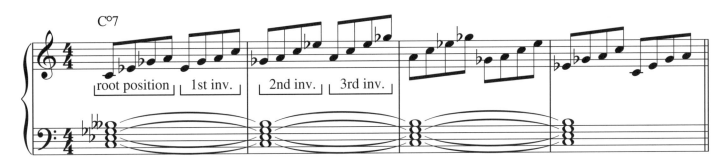

RHYTHM

Below is what we call the eighth-note grid. It indicates all the eighth notes possible in a measure of 4/4 time. Here are some things to keep in mind.

- Keep a quarter note pulse by beating your left hand on your left leg.
- Count aloud the rhythms above.
- Place a vocal accent on the four downbeats.

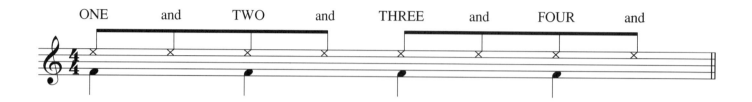

Eighth-note triplets are an integral part of jazz rhythmic language. Below is what we call the triplet grid. It indicates all the triplets possible in a measure of 4/4 time. Three eighth-note triplets fit into the space of one quarter note. Count aloud the three syllables "trip - o - let" to delineate the three parts of a single beat.

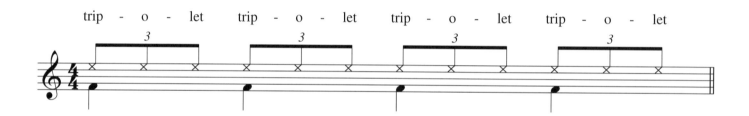

In jazz this triplet undercurrent is present throughout the music, lending it what we call a swing feel. This translates to eighth notes as well. The eighth notes are "swung," indicating that they should be played as the first and last notes of a triplet. In jazz we need to only write eighth notes, as it is understood that eighth notes are played this way. So when we see this written:

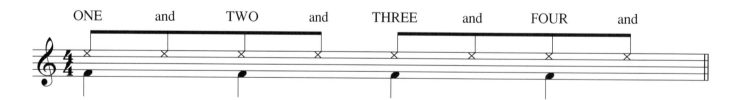

It actually sounds like this:

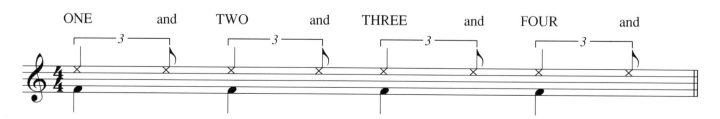

Dividing a quarter note into four equal parts produces sixteenth notes. Sixteenth notes are also an integral part of the improvisatory rhythmic language. Below we see the sixteenth note grid. Use the phrase "one e and a" to delineate the four parts of a single beat.

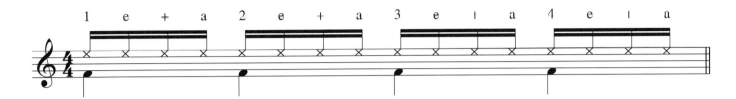

In bossa nova, Latin, or other straight-eighth feels, the eighth notes remain even, straight, and of equal duration. The basic two-bar rhythm underlying a Latin feel is written below. Play the two-bar rhythm with your right hand on your right leg against the steady quarter-note pulse of your left hand. Keep the eighth notes even (not swung), as if reading the rhythm in a classical piece of music.

THE ii–V–I PROGRESSION

In jazz we often identify a chord by its Roman numeral. The Roman numeral I refers to the tonic chord in the key in which we play a certain progression of chords. This enables us to transpose to different keys very easily. Below we see the diatonic 7th chords in the key of C.

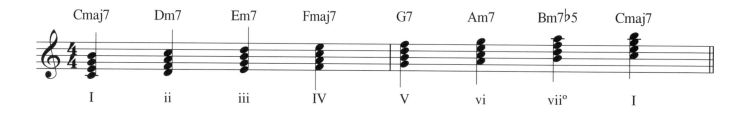

Similarly, here you see the I is now identifying the first chord in the key of F Major. Notice that the same Roman numerals are present, but now they are identifying chords in the key of F.

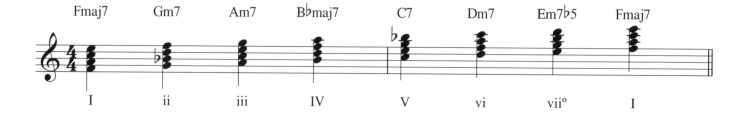

One of the most important series of chords in jazz is what we call the "two–five–one" progression. This progression is found in almost any written music. It consists of the ii, V, and I chord in any given key.

Below is a root-position ii–V–I progression in the key of C. Say the name of the chords aloud, substituting the Roman numeral for the key name. For example, say, "ii minor seven, V dominant seven, I major seven."

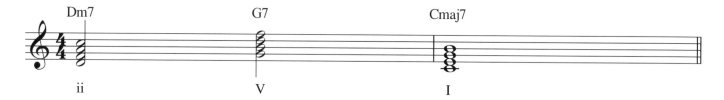

Play a root-position ii–V–I progression in each key through the cycle of 4ths. To help ground your ear, play the root of each chord in the left hand.

As we learned earlier, inversions allow us to play a series of chords with very little hand movement. By rearranging the order of notes it becomes very easy to move from one chord to the next. This results in smooth voice leading.

Below are some ii–V–I progressions that demonstrate how to make inversions work in this way. There are four possible inversions; play all of them through the cycle of 4ths. The first example begins with a root-position ii chord.

The second example begins with a first-inversion ii chord.

The third example begins with a second-inversion ii chord.

The fourth example begins with a third-inversion ii7 chord. It is the last of the four possible inversions.

The two most important notes in any given 7th chord are the 3rd and the 7th. The 3rd and the 7th tones determine quality—major or minor. Here is a simplified version of the ii–V–I progression that omits the 5th of each chord. Since the LH is playing the root, we'll exclude that from the RH as well to avoid doubling.

The first example begins with a root-position ii chord. Notice that the 7th of the chord is on the top to begin.

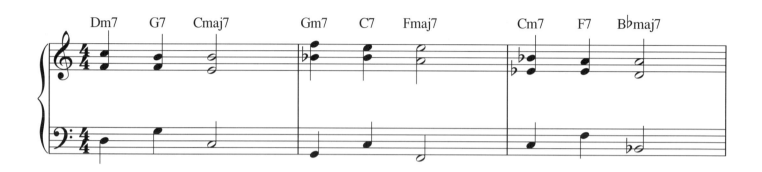

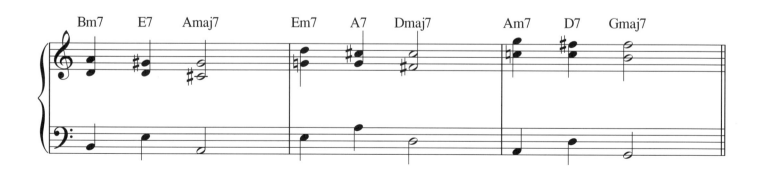

Now flip the tones so that the 3rd is on top to begin. Since we are only playing the 3rd and 7th, there are only two inversions for this exercise.

Now let's add some variety to the order in which we practice. Up to now we have used the cycle of 4ths to determine the root of the next key. We are now going to practice in two cycles of six keys.

In this example, the root of the I chord becomes the root of the ii chord for the next progression. This makes the progression descend in whole tones. After six whole steps the cycle starts to repeat itself. In the first cycle of six we cover the keys C, Bb, Ab, Gb, E, and D.

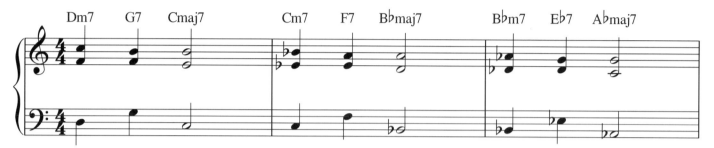

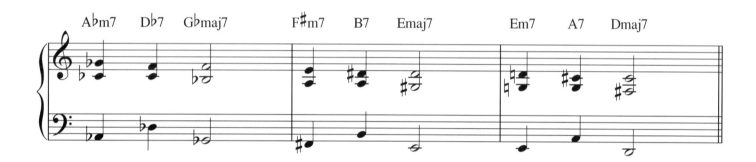

Now we will play through the remaining six keys. Begin by playing the next cycle of six a half step above where we started before. This time we cover the keys Db, B, A, G, F, and E.

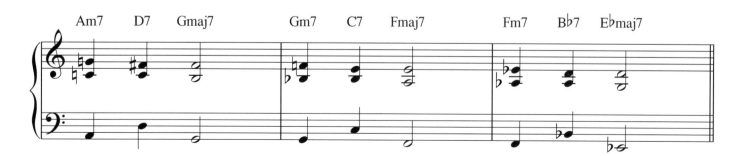

Now flip the 3rd and 7th and play through these two cycles again.

Try to practice these examples without the written music.

So far we've played all these 7th chords with just the root in the LH. By splitting up the four chord tones between hands, a more open sound is achieved, reminiscent of the Bach Chorales. Play through all four inversion pairings in two cycles of six. Arpeggiate each chord from the bottom up and identify the function of each tone.

Now put the 3rd and the 7th in the LH and the root and 5th in the RH.

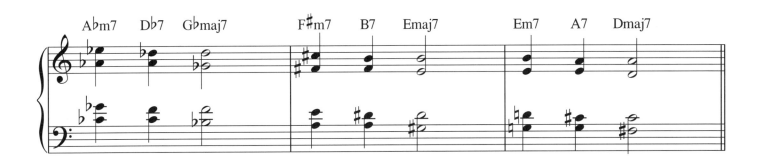

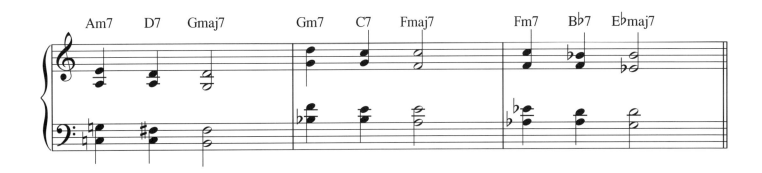

Now flip the root and 5th in the LH and put the 3rd and 7th in the RH.

Here's the last of the four possible inversions.

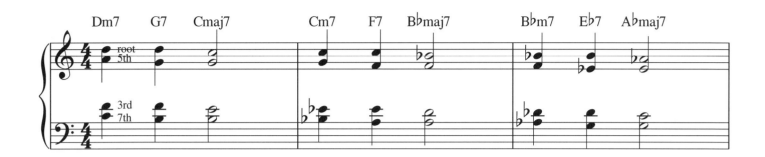

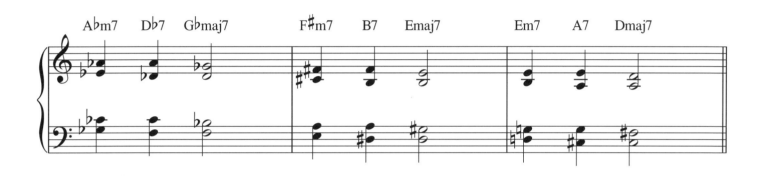

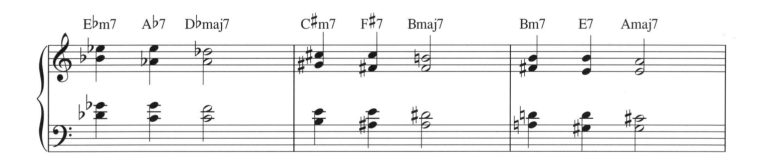

Below you will find some LH voicings for each ii–V–I progression. These voicings are generally used while a bassist is employed, leaving the RH free for improvisation. Therefore, several of the voicings are rootless, instead including the 9th or 13th. (More information on why these tensions can be used will be discussed in the following chapter.) Learning these LH voicings in all keys is a nonnegotiable issue for the improvising jazz pianist.

ALTERATIONS AND TENSIONS

Altering the 5th or the 7th tone will change or spice up the sound of a chord. However, by leaving the 3rd and 7th alone, the basic quality of the chord remains unchanged. Below are some examples of 7th chord alterations. Take these altered maj7 chords through their inversions in all keys.

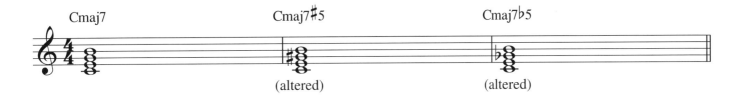

Take these altered dominant 7th chords through their inversions in all keys.

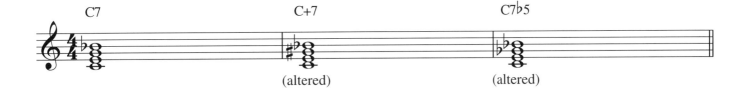

Altering the minor 7th chord by flatting the 5th produces a minor 7 flat 5 (m7♭5) chord. This is also known as a half-diminished chord, with which we are already familiar. The minor-major 7th chord is an extremely popular sound in jazz harmony. This chord is achieved by raising the ♭7th of a minor 7th chord to a major 7th. Although we have altered the 7th in this case, this chord still retains a primarily minor flavor due to the minor 3rd. Take these altered minor 7th chords through their inversions in all keys.

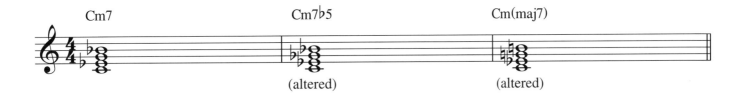

Another way to alter the sound of a chord is to add tensions to an already existing chord. Tensions are derived from the passing tones (the 2nd, 4th, and 6th tones) of a scale. They're used as extra notes above and beyond the basic chord tones (root, 3rd, 5th, and 7th). Therefore, we call them by their octave-derived numbers. The 2nd above the octave becomes the 9th, the 4th becomes the 11th, and the 6th becomes the 13th.

In a major 7th chord the appropriate tensions include the 9, ♯11, and 13.

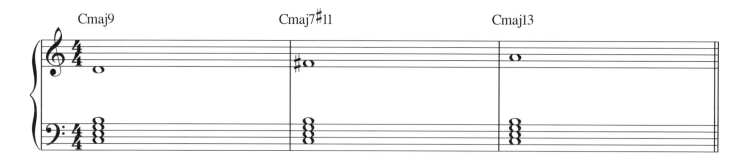

In a minor 7th chord the appropriate tensions include the 9, 11, and 13.

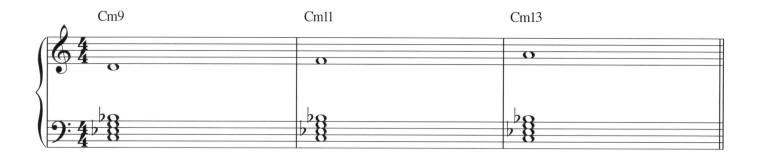

There are many tensions that sound appropriate on a dominant 7th chord. These tensions include the ♭9, ♮9, ♯9, ♯11, ♭13, and ♮13.

44

A great way to practice tensions is through arpeggiation. In the RH, arpeggiate the chord tones from the bottom up. Then in the next octave, arpeggiate all the appropriate tensions. For symmetry's sake, add another 9th before coming back down the octave in this example.

Arpeggiate all the major 7th chords and tensions through the cycle of 4ths. (You may notice that the tensions form a major triad on the 2nd degree of the key scale. For instance, the 9th, #11th, and 13th of Cmaj7 are D, F#, and A, respectively—a D major triad. This can be used to expedite the learning of these if it's easier for you.)

Now arpeggiate all the minor 7th chords and tensions through the cycle of 4ths. For symmetry's sake, add another 9th before coming back down the octave in this example as well. You may notice here that the tensions form a minor triad on the 2nd degree of the key scale.

Now arpeggiate all the dominant 7th chords and tensions through the cycle of 4ths. Remember to play a root-position 7th chord in the LH to ground your ear to the key you are playing in. The six tensions here do not form any triad—this one is tricky, so go slowly!

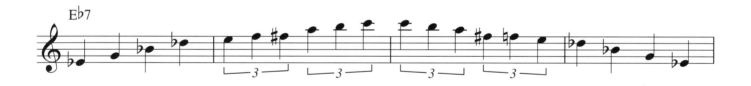

F#7

B7

E7

A7

D7

G7

UPPER STRUCTURE TRIADS

Tensions need not always be placed on top of the chord. In fact, tensions are most effectively utilized by incorporating them into the middle of the chord.

For a major 7th chord, the appropriate tensions are the 9th, ♯11th, and 13th. Notes to avoid are the 4th and the ♭7th. You may build a major triad on the 2nd and the 5th degrees of the key scale. Play each major 7th chord with an upper structure triad through the cycle of 4ths.

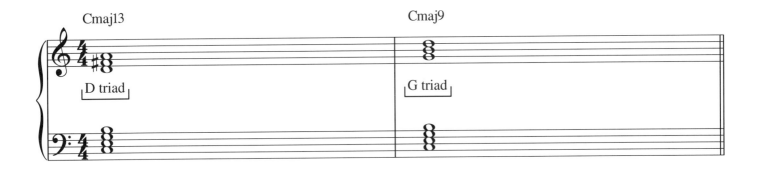

For a minor 7th chord, the appropriate tensions are the 9, 11, and 13. Notes to avoid are the major 3rd and the major 7th. You may build a major triad on the 4th and ♭7th degrees of the key scale. Play each minor 7th chord with an upper structure triad through the cycle of 4ths.

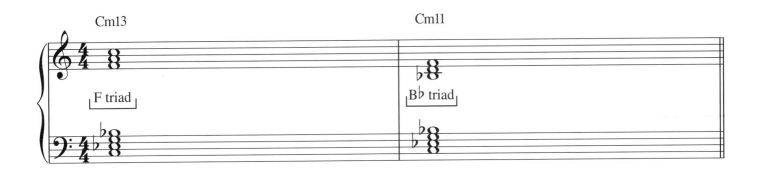

There are six tensions that will sound appropriate on a dominant 7th chord. These tensions include the ♭9th, ♮9th, ♯9th, ♯11th, ♭13th, and ♮13th. Notes to avoid are the 4th and the major 7th. You may build a major triad on the 2nd, ♭3rd, ♯4th, ♭6th, and ♮6th degrees of the key scale. Play each dominant 7th chord with an upper structure triad through the cycle of 4ths.

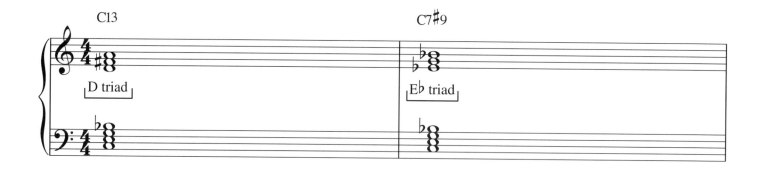

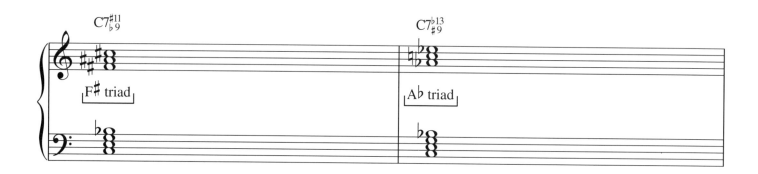

DIMINISHED SCALES AND CHORDS

A diminished scale is created by alternating whole steps and half steps from the root to the octave. There are two types of diminished scales.

- In a *whole-half* diminished scale, a whole step is the first interval played after the tonic.
- In a *half-whole* diminished scale, a half step is the first interval played after the tonic.

The whole-half scale works over a fully-diminished 7th chord. The half-whole scale works over an altered dominant 7th chord.

Play a C°7 chord in the LH, and run a whole-half diminished scale up and down in the RH.

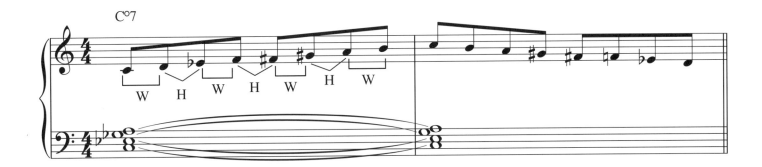

Play a C7 chord in the LH, and run a half-whole diminished scale up and down in the RH.

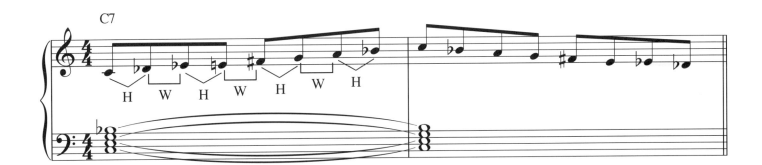

Because the diminished chord is built in minor 3rds it is known as a *symmetrical* chord. The diminished scale divides the octave into exactly four parts. Since twelve (the number of different notes) is divisible by three, there are three groups of four keys that share the same notes. Each root-position diminished 7th chord is the same as three other tonic key chords in their various inversions.

Group 1: C, E♭, F♯, and A diminished 7th chords all share the same notes.

Group 2: C♯, E, G, and A♯ diminished 7th chords all share the same notes.

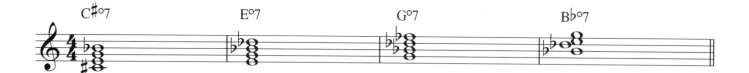

Group 3: D, F, A♭, and B diminished 7th chords all share the same notes.

There are only three different diminished scales. Although each scale begins on a different tone, the notes in each group are the same. It is still beneficial, however, to be able to begin the scale on each of the twelve keys.

Diminished scales can be broken down into two groups of four notes (tetrachords). Notice the first four notes of the C whole-half diminished scale (C–D–E♭–F). They are the same as the first four notes of an ascending C minor scale. The second four notes of the C whole-half diminished scale (F♯–G♯–A–B) are the same as the first four notes of an ascending F♯ minor scale. We can also see that a whole-half diminished scale is comprised of two tetrachords a tritone apart (in this case, C and F♯).

Play a diminished 7th chord in the LH, and run all the whole-half diminished scales up and down the octave in the RH.

Now let's practice the half-whole diminished scale. Notice the first four notes of the descending C half-whole diminished scale (C–B♭–A–G). They are the same as the first four notes of a descending C7 scale (or C Mixolydian mode). The second four notes of the C descending half-whole diminished scale (F♯–E–D♯–C♯) are the same as the first four notes of a descending F♯7 scale (F♯ Mixolydian mode). A half-whole diminished scale is also comprised of two tetrachords a tritone apart.

Play a dominant 7th chord in the LH, and run all the half-whole diminished scales up and down the octave in the RH. You may find it helpful to visualize in advance which accidentals go with which scale.

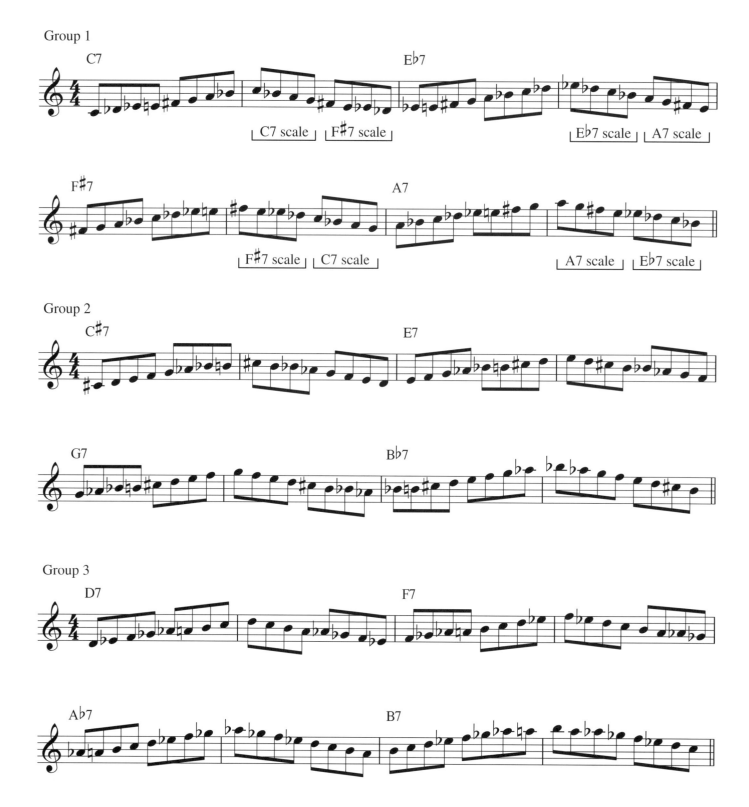

DROP 2 VOICINGS

One of the most important devices to utilize while playing jazz piano is a technique called drop 2. The 2 refers to the second note from the top of any given chord. Take the second note from the top and drop it from the RH, playing it an octave lower with the LH. The chord now becomes a two-handed voicing that you can employ while comping.

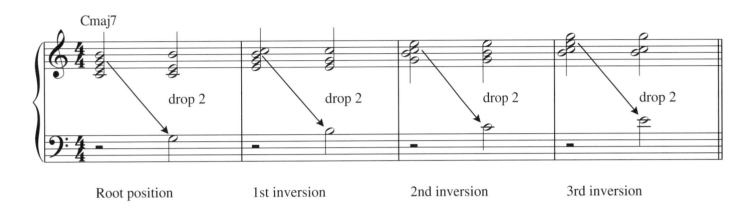

| Root position | 1st inversion | 2nd inversion | 3rd inversion |

The drop 2 technique works beautifully on diminished chords to harmonize passing tones. A fully diminished 7th chord is created by stacking a minor 3rd on top of an already diminished triad. Theoretically, a 7th chord must be written in 3rds. However, a diminished 7th chord often ends up with a double-flatted 7th (ex. C–E♭–G♭–B♭♭). Therefore, enharmonic labels are used for an easier visualization on some of the chords below.

So far we have practiced in all keys in two ways: the cycle of 4ths and two cycles of six. Practicing drop 2 diminished chords chromatically will prove extremely advantageous for comping. In preparation for drop 2, play these diminished chords up and down the chromatic scale.

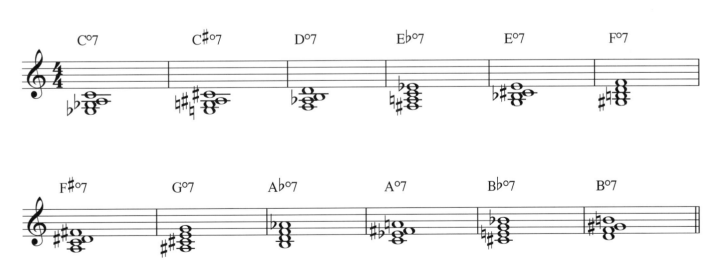

Now drop the second note from the top into the LH and play chromatically up and down the scale.

Discussed further in the next chapter, harmonizing a melody is a crucial skill in playing jazz piano. Being able to create a chord below any given melody note is imperative. A good way to practice this concept is to harmonize a scale. The notes in a scale can constitute a melody.

Below is a basic harmonization of a C major scale. The root, 3rd, and 5th are harmonized by a C6 or Cmaj7 chord. The passing tones (2nd, 4th, 6th, and 7th) are harmonized by utilizing diminished 7th chords. Play this harmonized melody based on a C major scale up and down the octave.

Now take the second note from the top and play it an octave lower with the LH.

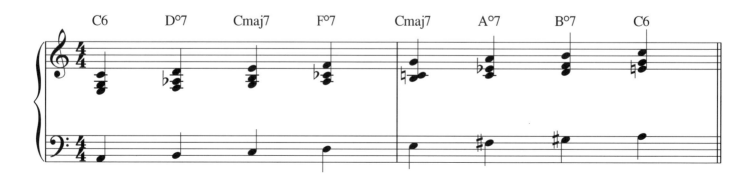

Let's continue to practice this concept by harmonizing a minor scale. For the purpose of this example we will use the C harmonic minor scale. Play this harmonized melody based on a C harmonic minor scale up and down the octave.

Now take the second note from the top and play it an octave lower with the LH.

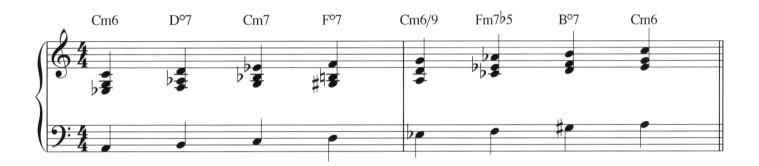

You have just successfully harmonized a melody utilizing the drop 2 technique!

HARMONIZING A MELODY

One of the most important skills to master in jazz is harmonizing a melody. Chords can be built below each melody note, determined by the chord symbol. The melody note will determine the chord's inversion. Here are some basic guidelines to consider.

*   The LH generally takes the root plus one or two other chord tones, such as the 3rd, 5th, or 7th.
*   The RH fills in with the other chord tones and tensions to embellish the sound of the chord.
*   Doubling chord tones between hands is usually avoided (except on a major 7th chord).

Let's try this technique out on a real song. Below are the first four bars to the ballad "The Safflower." First play the root of the chord in the LH. This will ground your ear to each melody note that you are harmonizing. Next determine the function of the melody note in relation to the chord symbol. Establishing the function of the melody note is the first and most important step.

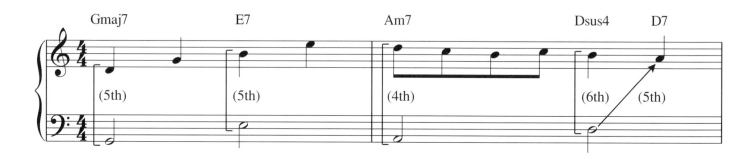

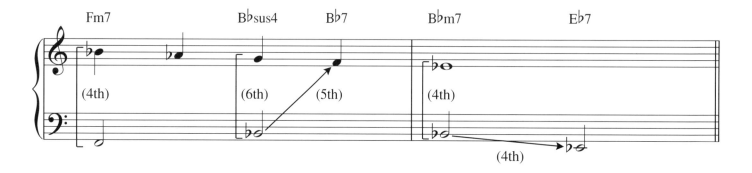

After you've determined each melody note's function, proceed to fill in the other chord tones and discretionary tensions. Play through the following written arrangement of "The Safflower" and analyze the function of each tone underneath the melody note.

Notice how the first chord is layered from the top down: 5th, 3rd, 9th, 7th, 5th, and root. All of the basic chord tones are present (root, 3rd, 5th, and 7th), and we've added one extension (9th). This makes for a nice full-sounding jazz chord.

THE SAFFLOWER

By SARAH JANE CION

APPROACH NOTES

Approach notes are an indispensable improvisational tool. Approach notes are tones that precede and/or surround a target note. The target note will almost always be a chord tone. There are many exercises to help facilitate the use of approach notes in improvisation. The first of these examples is called "half from below."

Play a major 7th chord in the LH. In the RH precede each chord tone by a half step from below. Go up and down the scale—always in the note order of one half step below the chord tone. Play the eighth notes as evenly as possible, as if you were playing a classical etude—slowly and deliberately. Play this exercise in all twelve keys through the cycle of 4ths.

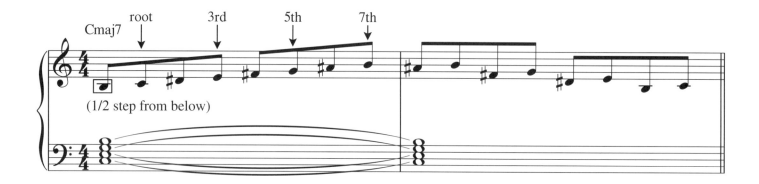

Now let's apply the same principle to dominant, minor, m7♭5, and diminished 7th chords. Continue to provide a LH root-position 7th chord for each example below and proceed through the twelve keys.

The next exercise is called "two from above." Here we approach each target note with two consecutive chromatic steps from above. Practice this on major, dominant, minor, m7♭5, and diminished 7th chords in all twelve keys.

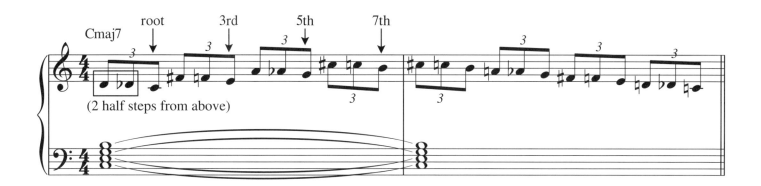

Continue to play a root-position 7th chord in the LH for each of these examples.

In this last exercise we combine the previous two examples. This hybrid example is called "two from above, half from below." Begin by approaching each target note with two consecutive chromatic steps from above. Then play a half step from below before finally playing the target note. Remember to play as slowly, steadily, and evenly as possible up and down the arpeggiated chord. Practice this on major, dominant, minor, m7♭5, and diminished 7th chords in all twelve keys.

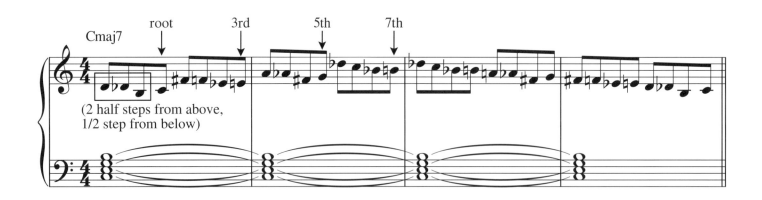

Continue to play a root-position 7th chord in the LH for each of these examples.

WALKING A BASS LINE

Walking a bass line in the LH simulates the role of an acoustic bass player, providing a solid accompaniment for yourself or others. A rudimentary bass line in 4/4 time consists of four quarter notes per measure. The root is almost always played on the first beat of each new chord symbol. Try to approach a new chord chromatically from above or below, or by its 5th or octave. Generally try to remain between C two octaves below middle C and the G below middle C.

Below is one way to construct a bass line on changes to the standard tune "Autumn Leaves."

To make the bass line sound a bit more authentic, the element of rhythm is added. This is done by judiciously placing two swing eighth notes in place of a quarter note. If the two eighth notes share the same tone, the first in the pair is played short and staccato. However, if the second note in the pair rocks back to the root, both notes are played legato. A pair of repeated notes are usually played on the first beat of a measure. Outlining chord tones by way of a triplet group is an effective way to adjust range.

Now let's add some RH chords that may be played over the LH bass line. Notice how many of the chords are often anticipated by an eighth note. This is one example of how a solo pianist might accompany an instrumentalist or singer.

12-BAR BLUES FORM

The blues is one of the most basic and important vehicles of improvisation in the jazz idiom. Hundreds and thousands of melodies (heads) have been written over the form of the blues. The blues is a 12-bar format that is based on a standard set of basic changes, although there are countless harmonic variations.

A basic blues consists of three dominant 7th chords—the I, IV, and V. Initially we will spend the majority of our practice time in the keys of C, F, B♭, and G. Eventually, however, one should practice the blues in all twelve keys.

Here is a basic blues in the key of C.

Version 1

Here is a variation that is a bit more adventuresome harmonically.

Version 2

Now let's look at some two-handed voicings for a blues in C. Notice how the top note remains within a relatively small intervallic range. This is a demonstration of good voice leading: the utilization of inversions to smooth the movement of voices from chord to chord.

Version 1

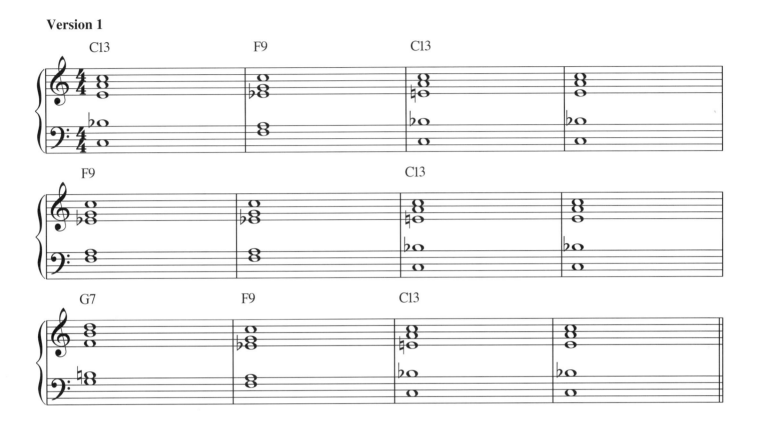

Arpeggiate each voicing from the bottom up and identify the function of each note.

Version 2

Play through each version of the blues in F several times.

Version 1

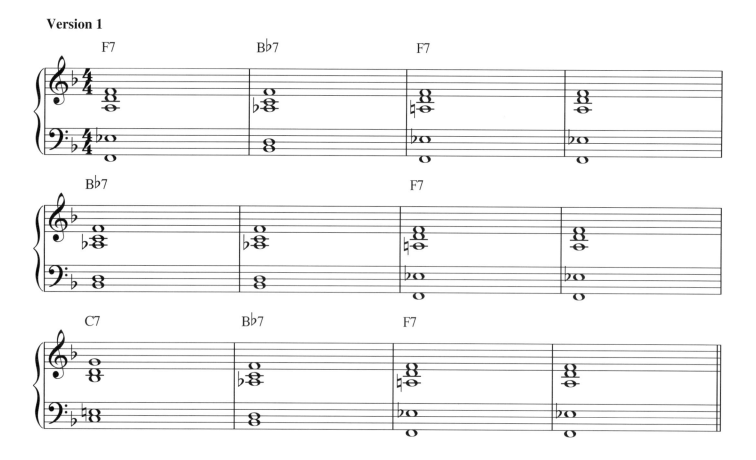

Commit these voicings to memory, and you'll fare well at any jam session.

Version 2

Now practice these voicings for the blues in B♭. What will make these voicings really come alive is rhythm.

Version 1

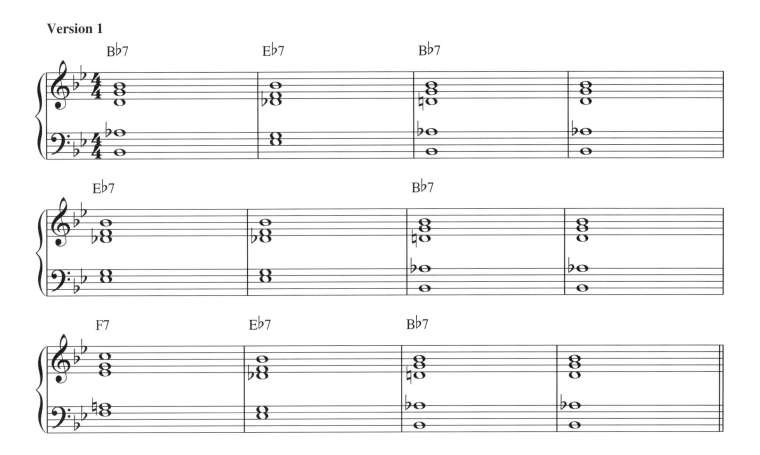

Mastery of two-handed voicings combined with the element of rhythm provides the fundamentals of comping.

Version 2

Notice that a typical lead sheet may only provide chord symbols reflecting basic 7th chords. Tensions are to be provided at the discretion of the pianist.

Version 1

You'll be in good shape by the time you've learned these blues voicings in G.

Version 2

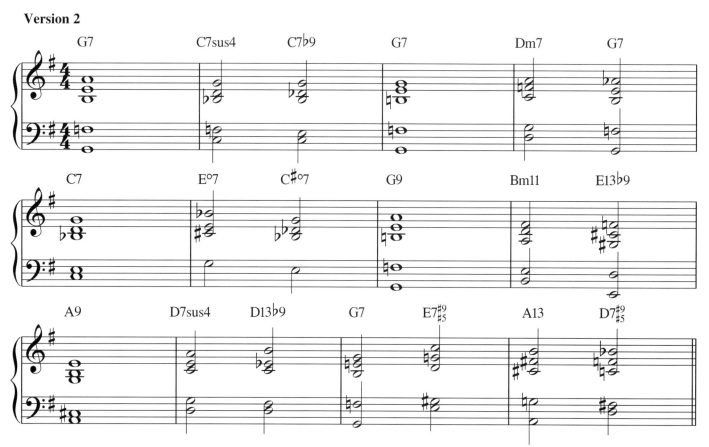

COMPING

In the language of jazz piano, comping is truly an art. The word "comping" is short for "accompanying." This is one of the most important skills to master in the scope of the craft.

When we comp we are accompanying a soloist with two-handed voicings. The rhythmic hits closely resemble what a drummer might play on his snare. The rhythms also resemble what an ensemble shout chorus might sound like in a big-band arrangement. Comping is a highly reactive function that should be done tastefully and often sparsely. It requires close listening so as to support the soloist—not overshadow or jumble the mix. Remember that the pianist is a rhythm section player and should work hard to blend with the ensemble.

Below is a rhythmic example of how a pianist might comp over a chorus of the blues. First get acquainted with the rhythmic aspect of the example. Set a tempo and clap on beats 2 and 4. Vocally articulate the rhythm over the 12-bar blues. It is vital to make the eighth notes swing during this exercise.

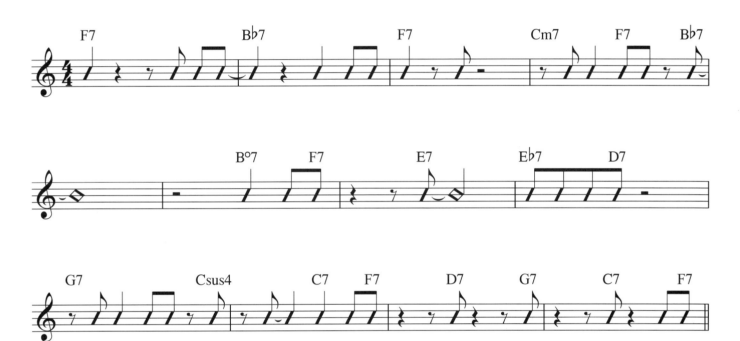

Combining rhythm with two-handed voicings creates accompaniment. While comping, a chord for the following measure is often anticipated by an eighth note tied over. Notice as well how there are various voicings that fit over a single chord. The top note will move around to create a little sub-melody that goes on underneath the soloist, or the middle note may move about chromatically to facilitate rhythmic and harmonic interest. Drop 2 voicings are another crucial ingredient in the primordial stew of comping.

Below is an example of what an experienced jazz pianist might play behind a soloist or singer for a blues in F. Set a metronome or tap your foot on beats 2 and 4 to a relaxed pace. Then practice the two-handed voicings four measures at a time. This example is particularly busy for the sake of demonstration. Remember that comping should be supportive, yet sparse.

LH comping is a technique used to accompany a RH solo. Generally speaking, it consists of short, staccato eighth-note jabs. LH voicings for blues are generally made from simple three-note voicings. Tunes that employ other kinds of 7th chords, however, will often employ three- or four-note voicings. Other than the first beat of a measure, LH comping rhythms are generally played in one of two ways:

- when the RH is resting or creating space;
- on the off beats.

Below is a LH rhythmic pattern that is a basic staple in jazz. Play through this blues chorus to get a feel for this rhythmic ostinato.

Now, play a simple riff in the RH while keeping the LH pattern going.

There are many variations on the LH rhythmic ostinato from the previous page. This rhythmic pattern is another staple that is often employed beneath a RH solo.

When playing solo piano, the LH is often treated differently from the way it would be if a bassist were present. Voicings tend to be more root-oriented when the pianist is playing alone. As well, when playing solo, LH note values are often extended. In general, however, the position of the LH comps will vary widely depending on how the melody or solo lies. The LH accompaniment complements the RH, often playing during the rests or off beats within a line.

Below is a melody based on the changes to the standard tune "Autumn Leaves." Visually see where the notes and rests in the melody coincide with the LH rhythms. The LH reflects the approach of a solo pianist.

FALL FOLIAGE

By SARAH JANE CION

HARMONIC VARIATIONS FOR BLUES

There are countless harmonic variations on the blues form. One popular variation is demonstrated by the tune "Blues for Alice" by Charlie Parker. This particular 12-bar progression is often referred to as "Blues for Alice" changes.

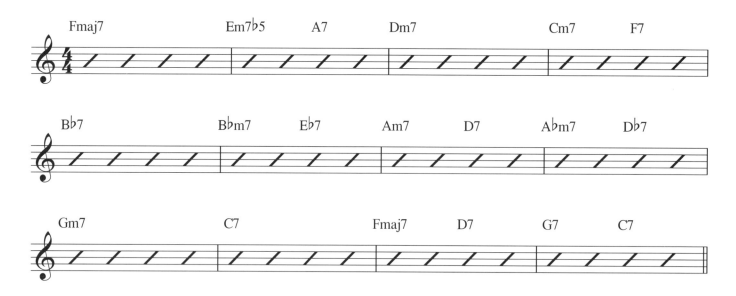

Below is an example of a melody based on the changes to "Blues for Alice." The LH illustrates comping that would be employed while playing with a bassist or trio.

SHOES FOR ALICE

By SARAH JANE CION

RHYTHM CHANGES

"Rhythm changes" is a term in jazz for a form based on the popular George Gershwin tune "I've Got Rhythm." It is a 32-bar AABA form consisting of an 8-bar A section and an 8-bar B section (the bridge).

The tune "Oleo" is an extremely popular rhythm-changes head that is played at jam sessions around the globe. The defining characteristic for this tune is that the bridge is improvised. Oftentimes the melodic instrumentalists will lay out on the B section, and the drummer will play unaccompanied.

Bebop melodies such as "Blues for Alice" and "Oleo" are great examples of composed improvisation. Below is a composition structured on rhythm changes. The LH assumes a bassist is engaged.

OLIVIO
(A NON-FAT BUTTER SPREAD)

By SARAH JANE CION

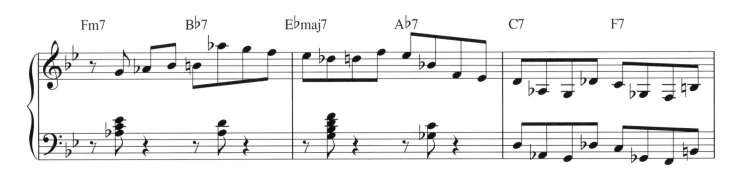

B

TRANSCRIPTIONS

Transcribing is a process vital to learning to play jazz. Nothing will help you understand, absorb, feel, and learn the language of jazz faster. Playing and studying transcriptions of solos is a great way to see how it's done. On the following pages you will find transcriptions of fifteen original tunes in the following various keys and feels:

Blues in C
Latin with a jazz/pop feel in A minor
Blues in F
Bluesy feel in D minor
Medium swing in B♭
Medium swing in B♭
Jazz waltz in E♭
Bluesy feel in C minor
Straight-eighth feel in A♭
Bluesy feel in F minor
Medium swing in D♭
Jazz Boogaloo in B
Blues in G
Bluesy feel in E minor
Jazz waltz in C

The melody may be changed or embellished slightly on the second A section and/or the head "out" following the solos. This is attributed to live performance in a studio setting, a common occurrence in a jazz format.

Here are some guidelines to help you practice with these tunes and transcriptions.

- Listen to each example while reading along with the transcription.
- Absorb the feel, phrasing, and dynamics of each example.
- Practice slowly without the recording first, and then play along with the recording.
- Try to make your solo indistinguishable from the solo on the CD.
- Try playing your own solo over the recording.
- Analyze the various intervallic relationships, chord scales, approach notes, and rhythms within each tune and solo.
- Extract some of your favorite licks or phrases from the solo and play them in all twelve keys.

Following these transcriptions you will find a list of some classic solos by jazz piano greats. When you feel ready, transcribe some solos on your own. The main objective is to mimic the phrasing, dynamics, and swing feel of the master players. Before long you will want to experience the joy of playing with a live rhythm section. Have fun and enjoy the journey!

CRUISIN'

By SARAH JANE CION

Blues in C ♩ = 118 (♫ = ♩♪)

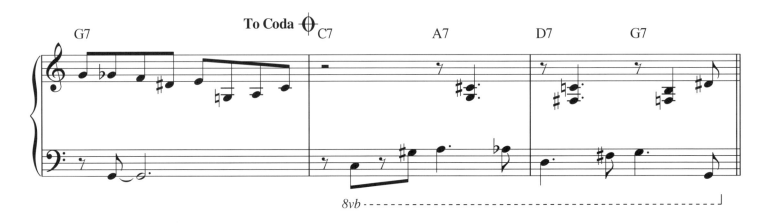

THE DOME

By SARAH JANE CION

PUSHIN' A BUGGY

By SARAH JANE CION

PRETTY KITTY

By SARAH JANE CION

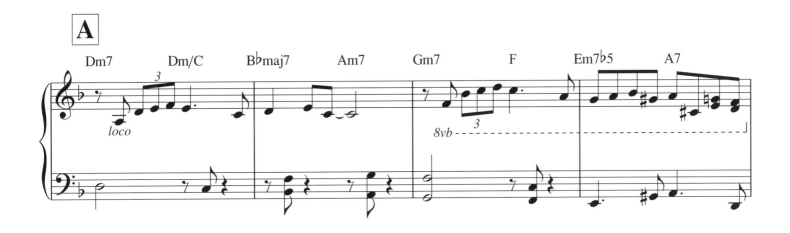

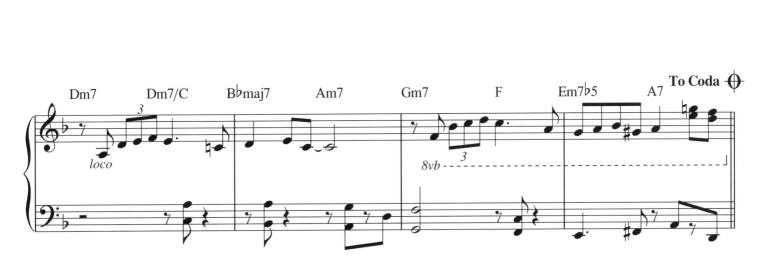

Solo

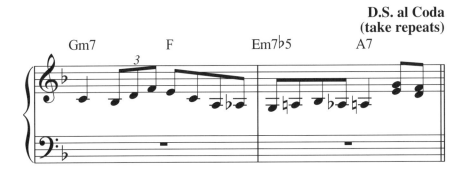

D.S. al Coda
(take repeats)

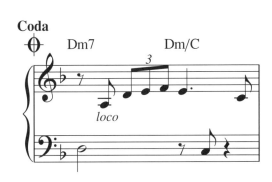

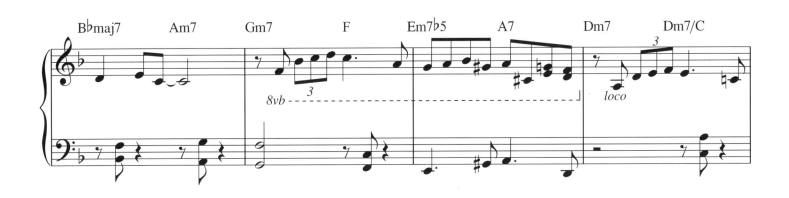

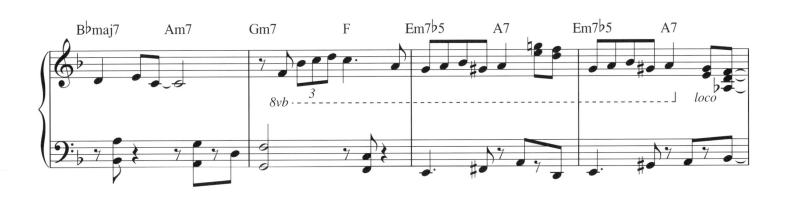

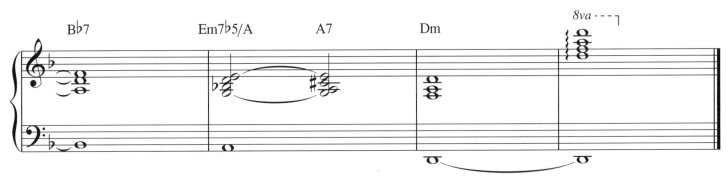

LOOK, I'M FLYING!

By SARAH JANE CION

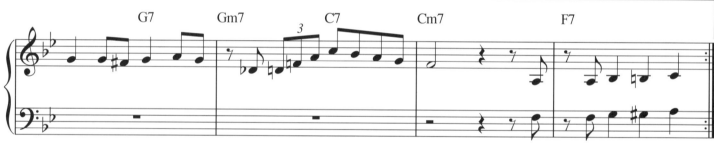

SQUISHY FISHY

By SARAH JANE CION

PLAYIN' PIANO

Track 7

By SARAH JANE CION

D.S. al Coda

Coda

CAT IN THE HAT

By SARAH JANE CION

Bluesy feel in C minor ♩ = 116

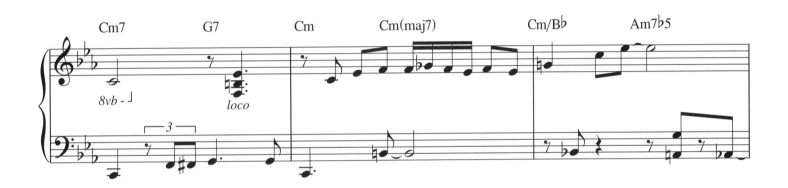

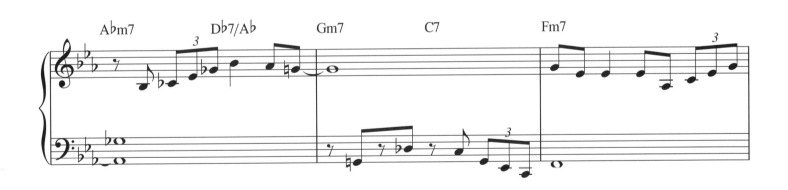

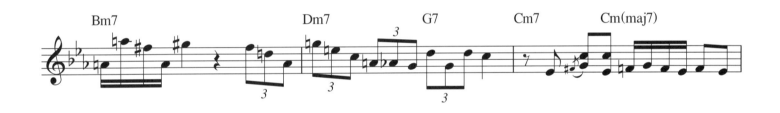

D.C. al Coda

Coda

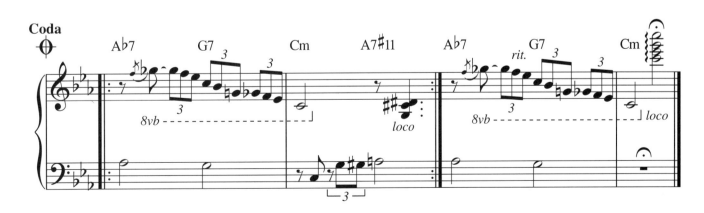

RHIANNA'S SONG

By SARAH JANE CION

*Freely arpeggiate chord

104

CRAWLIN'

By SARAH JANE CION

SUPER CUTE

By SARAH JANE CION

*Entire solo performed in 2-handed comping style.

D.C. al Coda
(take second ending)

THE HOBERMAN SPHERE

By SARAH JANE CION

*Freely arpeggiate chord

BATHTIME!

By SARAH JANE CION

114

A STARING CONTEST

By SARAH JANE CION

WALTZ FOR LARA

By SARAH JANE CION

APPENDIX
Tunes that All Jazz Musicians Should Know

Standards

It's You or No One
There Will Never Be Another You
I'll Remember April
Speak Low
What Is This Thing Called Love
Secret Love
How High the Moon
Just Friends
Love for Sale
Falling in Love with Love
Cherokee
My Shining Hour
The Way You Look Tonight
The Song Is You
You Stepped out of a Dream
Just One of Those Things
Just in Time
Lover
The Night Has 1000 Eyes
If I Were a Bell
What Am I Here For
Strike Up the Band
The End of a Love Affair
Bye Bye Blackbird
From This Moment On
I Get a Kick out of You
Old Devil Moon
After You've Gone
Get Happy
That's All
It's All Right with Me
I Remember You
This Could Be the Start of
      Something Big
All or Nothing at All
So in Love
I'm Getting Sentimental over You
All the Things You Are
There Is No Greater Love
Night and Day
I Hear a Rhapsody
Stella by Starlight
Green Dolphin Street
Autumn Leaves
Have You Met Miss Jones

Lullaby of Birdland
Out of Nowhere
Star Eyes
I Love You
Four
Just You Just Me
Summertime
Gone with the Wind
Our Love Is Here to Stay
I'm Confessin'
Stompin' at the Savoy
Shiny Stockings
But Not for Me
The Masquerade is Over
East of the Sun
The More I See You
You're My Everything
I'm an Old Cowhand
All of You
It Could Happen to You
I Could Write a Book
Spring is Here
Witchcraft
If I Should Lose You
April in Paris
The Best Thing for You is Me
Manhattan
September in the Rain
I Didn't Know What Time It Was
How Deep is the Ocean
I Thought About You
Come Rain or Come Shine
Yesterdays
Easy to Love
Alone Together
Sweet and Lovely
I'm Old Fashioned
Long Ago and Far Away
Dream Dancing
Days of Wine and Roses
On the Street Where You Live
Sweet Lorraine
I Concentrate on You
You and the Night and the Music
I Cover the Waterfront
Too Marvelous for Words
Softly, as in a Morning Sunrise
Without a Song

Let's Get Lost
This I Dig of You
Isfahan
Sweet Georgia Brown
Indiana
S'Wonderful
Love Me or Leave Me
Savoy
Cheek to Cheek
Easy to Love

Ballads

I'll Be Seeing You
What's New
I Should Care
Body and Soul
My Ideal
Darn that Dream
Beautiful Love
My Old Flame
Every Time We Say Goodbye
For All We Know
Tenderly
You've Changed
You Go to My Head
Where Are You
Stardust
Smoke Gets in Your Eyes
You Don't Know What Love Is
Some Other Time
When Your Lover Has Gone
Polka Dots and Moonbeams
If I Had You
Easy Living
Laura
If You Could See Me Now
We'll Be Together Again
Willow Weep for Me
Autumn in New York
Old Folks
My One and Only Love
Why Did I Choose You
More Than you Know
I Can't Get Started
Ghost of a Chance

Embraceable You
Skylark
The Nearness of You
If I Should Lose You
My Foolish Heart
My Romance
My Ideal
But Beautiful
Everything I Have Is Yours
Peace
Ask Me Now
Prelude to a Kiss
Sophisticated Lady
Lush Life
In a Sentimental Mood
A Child Is Born
Blue in Green
God Bless the Child
I Should Care
In My Solitude
Spring Is Here
Sophisticated Lady

Bossa Novas

Invitation
Con Alma
Ceora
Blue Bossa
Poinciana
Saint Thomas
Recordame
Nica's Dream
Song for My Father
It Might as Well Be Spring
The Shadow of Your Smile
Wave
Corcovado
Meditation
Girl From Ipanema
Triste
Watch What Happens
How Insensitive
Besame Mucho

Waltzes

Someday My Prince Will Come
Bluesette
A Child Is Born
Up Jumped Spring
Footprints
All Blues
My Favorite Things
Tenderly
Waltz for Debbie
Alice in Wonderland
Emily

Falling in Love with Love

Bebop

Lazy Bird
Giant Steps
Tune Up
Pent-Up House
Dig
Minority
Woody 'n' You
Quicksilver
Jeanine
Dahoud
This I Dig of You
Hot House
Groovin' High
Doxy
Fried Bananas
Strollin'
Joy Spring
Oleo
In Your Own Sweet Way
A Night in Tunisia
Celia
Solar
Milestones
Old Milestones
Donna Lee
Ornithology
Confirmation
Quasimodo
Yardbird Suite
Anthropology
Airegin

Monk

Blue Monk
Straight, No Chaser
Hackensack
'Round Midnight
Ruby My Dear
Eronel
Rhythm-a-ning
Evidence
Well You Needn't
I Mean You
In Walked Bud
Ask Me Now
Let's Cool One
Pannonica

Duke Ellington

Perdido
Solitude

In a Mellow Tone
Take the A Train
Don't Get Around Much Anymore
Caravan
Satin Doll
Sophisticated Lady
In a Sentimental Mood
Solitude
I Got It Bad
Mood Indigo
I Let a Song Go out of My Heart
Lush Life
Isfahan

Trane/Post Bop

Moments Notice
Lazybird
Giant Steps
Milestones
Stablemates
Whisper Not
The Cupbearers
Firm Roots
Bolivia
One Finger Snap
Black Nile
Inner Urge
Along Came Betty
Sugar
Maiden Voyage
So What
Impressions
Dolphin Dance
Witch Hunt
Little Sunflower
Peri's Scope
The Duke
Beatrice

Blues

Blue Monk
Tenor Madness
Byrd-Like
Walkin'
Cheryl
Sandu
Billy's Bounce
Au Privave
Blues in the Corner
Mr. P.C.
Moanin'
Blues for Alice

Great Jazz Pianists to Check Out

Monty Alexander
Kenny Barron
JoAnne Brackeen
Donald Brown
Joey Calderazzo
Michel Camilo
Bill Charlap
Sonny Clark
Chick Corea
Harold Danko
Kenny Drew
Eliane Elias
Bill Evans
Tommy Flanagan
Hal Galper
Red Garland

Larry Goldings
Benny Green
Herbie Hancock
Barry Harris
Gene Harris
Fred Hersch
Ahmad Jamal
Keith Jarrett
Hank Jones
Wynton Kelly
Geoff Keezer
Kenny Kirkland
Andy LaVerne
Mike Longo
Jim McNeely
Brad Mehldau

Mulgrew Miller
Thelonius Monk
Phineas Newborn, Jr.
Danilo Perez
Oscar Peterson
Bud Powell
Ted Rosenthal
Renee Rosnes
George Shearing
Horace Silver
Bobby Timmons
McCoy Tyner
Chucho Valdez
Cedar Walton
James Williams

Classic Solos to Check out and Transcribe

Pianist	Song	Album
Kenny Barron	"Evidence"	*Four in One*–Sphere
JoAnne Brackeen	"Solar"	*New True Illusion*
JoAnne Brackeen	"My Romance"	*New True Illusion*
Chick Corea	"Steps-What Was"	*Now He Sings, Now He Sobs*
Chick Corea	"Matrix"	*Now He Sings, Now He Sobs*
Chick Corea	"Crystal Silence"	*Crystal Silence*
Kenny Drew	"Moments Notice"	*Blue Trane*–John Coltrane
Bill Evans	"My Romance"	*Intuition*
Bill Evans	"Green Dolphin Street"	*Tokyo Concert*
Tommy Flannagan	"I Love You"	*Super Session*
Larry Goldings	"Hit and Run"	*On Course*
Herbie Hancock	"One Finger Snap"	*Empyrean Isles*
Herbie Hancock	"Dolphin Dance"	*Maiden Voyage*
Herbie Hancock	"Stella by Starlight"	*My Funny Valentine*–Miles Davis
Herbie Hancock	"All of You"	*My Funny Valentine*–Miles Davis
Gene Harris	"Yours is My Heart Alone"	*Trio Plus One*
Keith Jarrett	"My Romance"	*Buttercorn Lady*–Art Blakey
Wynton Kelly	"Someday My Prince Will Come"	*Someday My Prince Will Come*–Miles Davis
Thelonious Monk	"Off Minor"	*Monk and Trane*
Phineas Newborn	"Dahoud"	*A World of Piano*
Oscar Peterson	"Blues Etude"	*Blues Etude*
Bud Powell	"Bouncin' with Bud"	*The Amazing Bud Powell Vol.1*
Bobby Timmons	"Moanin'"	*Moanin'*–Art Blakey
McCoy Tyner	"Speak Low"	*Inception*
McCoy Tyner	"Woody 'n' You"	*Live at Newport*
McCoy Tyner	"Passion Dance"	*The Real McCoy*

ABOUT THE AUTHOR

Sarah Jane Cion was the First place winner of the internationally acclaimed 17th Annual Great American Jazz Piano Competition held in Jacksonville Florida on November 11th, 1999; and was a featured guest on the nationally syndicated NPR radio show Piano Jazz with Marian McPartland.

Sarah has performed with young and older jazz greats such as Clark Terry, Etta Jones, Anita O'Day, Della Griffin, Ralph Lalama, Allan Harris, Carmen Leggio, and many others. She is currently performing with best-selling author and tenor man James McBride. Her debut CD *Indeed!* features alto saxophonist Antonio Hart and drummer Tony Reedus. Her second release, *Moon Song*, on the Naxos Jazz label, features bassist Phil Palombi, tenor man Chris Potter, and Billy Hart. Her third CD, *Summer Night*, features saxophone giant Michael Brecker.

Cion's articles and transcriptions have been published in Piano Today Magazine. Her original song "It's Christmas Time, Once Again" was a finalist in the internationally acclaimed 1997 John Lennon Songwriting Contest, and Cion's music is currently being featured on the WABC TV soap *All My Children*.

Sarah graduated from the New England Conservatory in 1990 with honors and distinction in composition and performance. She lives in Riverdale, NY, with her husband, bassist Phil Palombi, and daughter Lara Gabrielle.

NOTE-FOR-NOTE KEYBOARD TRANSCRIPTIONS

These outstanding collections feature note-for-note transcriptions from the artists who made the songs famous.
No matter what style you play, these books are perfect for performers or students who want to play just like their keyboard idols.

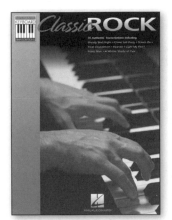

CLASSIC ROCK

Authentic transcriptions – right off the recordings! – of these 35 all-time rock classics: Beth • Bloody Well Right • Changes • Cold as Ice • Come Sail Away • Don't Do Me Like That • Green-Eyed Lady • Hard to Handle • Heaven • Killer Queen • King of Pain • Lady Madonna • Layla • Light My Fire • Oye Como Va • Piano Man • Takin' Care of Business • Werewolves of London • Woman from Tokyo • and more.

00310940
$24.95

THE CAROLE KING KEYBOARD BOOK

Note-for-note transcriptions of all the piano and keyboard parts on 16 of King's greatest songs: Beautiful • Been to Canaan • Home Again • I Feel the Earth Move • It's Too Late • Jazzman • (You Make Me Feel) Like a Natural Woman • Nightingale • Smackwater Jack • So Far Away • Sweet Seasons • Tapestry • Way Over Yonder • Where You Lead • Will You Love Me Tomorrow • You've Got a Friend.

00690554
$19.95

JAZZ

Authentic note-for-note transcriptions of 24 favorites from jazz piano masters including Bill Evans, Thelonious Monk, Oscar Peterson, Bud Powell, and Art Tatum. Includes: Ain't Misbehavin' • April in Paris • Autumn in New York • Body and Soul • Freddie Freeloader • Giant Steps • My Foolish Heart • My Funny Valentine • Satin Doll • Song for My Father • Stella by Starlight • and more.

00310941
$22.95

POP/ROCK

35 note-for-note transcriptions for those who want to play *exactly* what they hear on recordings. Songs include: Africa • Against All Odds • Axel F • Centerfold • Chariots of Fire • Cherish • Don't Let the Sun Go Down on Me • Drops of Jupiter (Tell Me) • Faithfully • It's Too Late • Just the Way You Are • Let It Be • Mandy • Sailing • Sweet Dreams Are Made of This • Walking in Memphis.

00310939
$24.95

THE BILLY JOEL KEYBOARD BOOK

A new addition to our popular Note-for-Note Keyboard Transcriptions series, this beauty features 16 megahits from the Piano Man himself! Includes: Allentown • And So It Goes • Honesty • Just the Way You Are • Movin' Out • My Life • New York State of Mind • Piano Man • Pressure • She's Got a Way • Tell Her About It • and more.

00694828
$22.95

R&B

Exact transcriptions straight from the recordings of 35 R&B classics: Baby Love • Boogie on Reggae Woman • Easy • Endless Love • Fallin' • Green Onions • Higher Ground • I'll Be There • Just Once • Money (That's What I Want) • On the Wings of Love • Ribbon in the Sky • This Masquerade • Three Times a Lady.

00310942
$24.95

Visit Hal Leonard online at **www.halleonard.com**

FOR MORE INFORMATION, SEE YOUR LOCAL MUSIC DEALER,
OR WRITE TO:

HAL•LEONARD®
CORPORATION
7777 W. BLUEMOUND RD. P.O. BOX 13819 MILWAUKEE, WI 53213

Prices, contents and availability subject to change without notice.

0804

Presenting the Hal Leonard JAZZ PLAY ALONG SERIES

DUKE ELLINGTON Vol. 1 00841644
Caravan • Don't Get Around Much Anymore • In a Mellow Tone • In a Sentimental Mood • It Don't Mean a Thing (If It Ain't Got That Swing) • Perdido • Prelude to a Kiss • Satin Doll • Sophisticated Lady • Take the "A" Train.

MILES DAVIS Vol. 2 00841645
All Blues • Blue in Green • Four • Half Nelson • Milestones • Nardis • Seven Steps to Heaven • So What • Solar • Tune Up.

THE BLUES Vol. 3 00841646
Billie's Bounce • Birk's Works • Blues for Alice • Blues in the Closet • C-Jam Blues • Freddie Freeloader • Mr. P.C. • Now's the Time • Tenor Madness • Things Ain't What They Used to Be.

JAZZ BALLADS Vol. 4 00841691
Body and Soul • But Beautiful • Here's That Rainy Day • Misty • My Foolish Heart • My Funny Valentine • My One and Only Love • My Romance • The Nearness of You.

BEST OF BEBOP Vol. 5 00841689
Anthropology • Donna Lee • Doxy • Epistrophy • Lady Bird • Oleo • Ornithology • Scrapple from the Apple • Woodyn' You • Yardbird Suite.

**JAZZ CLASSICS WITH EASY CHANGES
Vol. 6** 00841690
Blue Train • Comin' Home Baby • Footprints • Impressions • Killer Joe • Moanin' • Sidewinder • St. Thomas • Stolen Moments • Well You Needn't.

**ESSENTIAL JAZZ STANDARDS
Vol. 7** 00843000
Autumn Leaves • Cotton Tail • Easy Living • I Remember You • If I Should Lose You • Lullaby of Birdland • Out of Nowhere • Stella by Starlight • There Will Never Be Another You • When Sunny Gets Blue.

**ANTONIO CARLOS JOBIM AND
THE ART OF THE BOSSA NOVA
Vol. 8** 00843001
The Girl from Ipanema • How Insensitive • Meditation • Once I Loved • One Note Samba • Quiet Nights of Quiet Stars • Slightly Out of Tune • So Danco Samba • Triste • Wave.

DIZZY GILLESPIE Vol. 9 00843002
Birk's Works • Con Alma • Groovin' High • Manteca • A Night in Tunisia • Salt Peanuts • Shawnuff • Things to Come • Tour De Force • Woodyn' You.

DISNEY CLASSICS Vol. 10 00843003
Alice in Wonderland • Beauty and the Beast • Cruella De Vil • Heigh-Ho • Some Day My Prince Will Come • When You Wish upon a Star • Whistle While You Work • Who's Afraid of the Big Bad Wolf • You've Got a Friend in Me • Zip-a-Dee-Doo-Dah.

**RODGERS AND HART FAVORITES
Vol. 11** 00843004
Bewitched • The Blue Room • Dancing on the Ceiling • Have You Met Miss Jones? • I Could Write a Book • The Lady Is a Tramp • Little Girl Blue • My Romance • There's a Small Hotel • You Are Too Beautiful.

**ESSENTIAL JAZZ CLASSICS
Vol. 12** 00843005
Airegin • Ceora • The Frim Fram Sauce • Israel • Milestones • Nefertiti • Red Clay • Satin Doll • Song for My Father • Take Five.

JOHN COLTRANE Vol. 13 00843006
Blue Train • Countdown • Cousin Mary • Equinox • Giant Steps • Impressions • Lazy Bird • Mr. P.C. • Moment's Notice • Naima.

IRVING BERLIN Vol. 14 00843007
Be Careful, It's My Heart • Blue Skies • Change Partners • Cheek to Cheek • I've Got My Love to Keep Me Warm • Steppin' Out with My Baby • They Say It's Wonderful • What'll I Do?

**RODGERS & HAMMERSTEIN
Vol. 15** 00843008
Bali Ha'i • Do I Love You Because You're Beautiful? • Hello Young Lovers • I Have Dreamed • It Might as Well Be Spring • Love, Look Away • My Favorite Things • The Surrey with the Fringe on Top • The Sweetest Sounds • Younger Than Springtime.

COLE PORTER Vol. 16 00843009
All of You • At Long Last • Easy to Love • Ev'ry Time We Say Goodbye • I Concentrate on You • I've Got You Under My Skin • In the Still of the Night • It's All Right with Me • It's De-Lovely • You'd Be So Nice to Come Home To.

COUNT BASIE Vol. 17 00843010
All of Me • April in Paris • Blues in Hoss Flat • Cute • Jumpin' at the Woodside • Li'l Darlin' • Moten Swing • One O'Clock Jump • Shiny Stockings • Until I Met You.

HAROLD ARLEN Vol. 18 00843011
Ac-cent-tchu-ate the Positive • Between the Devil and the Deep Blue Sea • Come Rain or Come Shine • If I Only Had a Brain • It's Only a Paper Moon • I've Got the World on a String • My Shining Hour • Over the Rainbow • Stormy Weather • That Old Black Magic.

COOL JAZZ Vol. 19 00843012
Bernie's Tune • Boplicity • Budo • Conception • Django • Five Brothers • Line for Lyons • Walkin' Shoes • Waltz for Debby • Whisper Not.

**RODGERS AND HART CLASSICS
Vol. 21** 00843014
Falling in Love with Love • Isn't it Romantic? • Manhattan • Mountain Greenery • My Funny Valentine • My Heart Stood Still • This Can't Be Love • Thou Swell • Where or When • You Took Advantage of Me.

WAYNE SHORTER Vol. 22 00843015
Children of the Night • ESP • Footprints • Juju • Mahjong • Nefertiti • Nightdreamer • Speak No Evil • Witch Hunt • Yes and No.

LATIN JAZZ Vol. 23 00843016
Agua De Beber • Chega De Saudade • The Gift! • Invitation • Manha De Carnaval • Mas Que Nada • Ran Kan Kan • So Nice • Sweet Happy Life • Watch What Happens.

**EARLY JAZZ STANDARDS
Vol. 24** 00843017
After You've Gone • Avalon • Indian Summer • Indiana (Back Home Again in Indiana) • Ja-Da • Limehouse Blues • Paper Doll • Poor Butterfly • Rose Room • St. Louis Blues.

CHRISTMAS JAZZ Vol. 25 00843018
The Christmas Song (Chestnuts Roasting on an Open Fire) • The Christmas Waltz • Frosty the Snow Man • Home for the Holidays • I Heard the Bells on Christmas Day • I'll Be Home for Christmas • Let It Snow! Let It Snow! Let It Snow! • Rudolph the Red-Nosed Reindeer • Silver Bells • Snowfall.

CHARLIE PARKER Vol. 26 00843019
Au Privave • Billie's Bounce • Confirmation • Donna Lee • Moose the Mooche • My Little Suede Shoes • Now's the Time • Ornithology • Scrapple from the Apple • Yardbird Suite.

**GREAT JAZZ STANDARDS
Vol. 27** 00843020
Fly Me to the Moon • Girl Talk • How High the Moon • I Can't Get Started with You • It Could Happen to You • Lover • Softly As in a Morning Sunrise • Speak Low • Tangerine • Willow Weep for Me.

BIG BAND ERA Vol. 28 00843021
Air Mail Special • Christopher Columbus • Four Brothers • In the Mood • Intermission Riff • Jersey Bounce • Opus One • Stompin' at the Savoy • A String of Pearls • Tuxedo Junction.

**LENNON AND MCCARTNEY
Vol. 29** 00843022
And I Love Her • Blackbird • Come Together • Eleanor Rigby • The Fool on the Hill • Here, There and Everywhere • Lady Madonna • Let It Be • Ticket to Ride • Yesterday.

BLUES BEST Vol. 30 00843023
Basin Street Blues • Bloomdido • D Natural Blues • Everyday I Have the Blues Again • Happy Go Lucky Local • K.C. Blues • Sonnymoon for Two • The Swingin' Shepherd Blues • Take the Coltrane • Turnaround.

JAZZ IN THREE Vol. 31 00843024
Bluesette • Gravy Waltz • Jitterbug Waltz • Moon River • Oh, What a Beautiful Mornin' • Tenderly • Tennessee Waltz • West Coast Blues • What the World Needs Now Is Love • Wives and Lovers.

BEST OF SWING Vol. 32 00843025
Alright, Okay, You Win • Cherokee • I'll Be Seeing You • I've Heard That Song Before • Java Jive • Jump, Jive An' Wail • On the Sunny Side of the Street • Route 66 • Sentimental Journey • What's New?

SONNY ROLLINS Vol. 33 00843029
Airegin • Alfie's Theme • Biji • Doxy • Here's to the People • Oleo • St. Thomas • Sonnymoon for Two.

ALL TIME STANDARDS Vol. 34 00843030
Autumn in New York • Bye Bye Blackbird • Call Me Irresponsible • Georgia on My Miind • Honeysuckle Rose • I'll Remember April • Stardust • There Is No Greater Love • The Very Thought of You • Broadway.

BLUESY JAZZ Vol. 35 00843031
Angel Eyes • Bags' Groove • Bessie's Blues • Chitlins Con Carne • Good Morning Heartache • High Fly • Mercy, Mercy, Mercy • Night Train • Sugar • Sweet Georgia Bright.

HORACE SILVER Vol. 36 00843032
Doodlin' • The Jody Grind • Nica's Dream • Peace • The Preacher • Senor Blues • Sister Sadie • Song for My Father • Strollin'.

BILL EVANS Vol. 37 00843033
Funkallero • My Bells • One for Helen • The Opener • Orbit • Show-Type Tune • 34 Skidoo • Time Remembered • Turn Out the Stars • Waltz for Debby.

YULETIDE JAZZ Vol. 38 00843034
Blue Christmas • Christmas Time Is Here • Feliz Navidad • Happy Holiday • Here Comes Santa Claus • A Marshmallow World • Merry Christmas, Darling • The Most Wonderful Time of the Year • My Favorite Things • Santa Claus Is Comin' to Town.

**ALL THE THINGS YOU ARE & MORE
JEROME KERN SONGS
Vol. 39** 00843035
All the Things You Are • Can't Help Lovin' Dat Man • Dearly Beloved • A Fine Romance • The Folks Who Live on the Hill • Long Ago (And Far Away) • Pick Yourself Up • The Song Is You • The Way You Look Tonight • Yesterday.

BOSSA NOVA Vol. 40 00843036
Black Orpheus • Call Me • Dindi • Little Boat • A Man and a Woman • Only Trust Your Heart • The Shadow of Your Smile • Song of the Jet (Samba do Aviao) • Watch What Happens • Wave.

**CLASSIC DUKE ELLINGTON
Vol. 41** 00843037
C-Jam Blues • Come Sunday • Cotton Tail • Do Nothin' Till You Hear from Me • I Got It Bad and That Ain't Good • I Let a Song Go Out of My Heart • I'm Beginning to See the Light • I'm Just a Lucky So and So • Mood Indigo • Solitude.

**GERRY MULLIGAN FAVORITES
Vol. 42** 00843038
Bark for Barksdale • Dragonfly • Elevation • Idol Gossip • Jeru • The Lonely Night (Night Lights) • Noblesse • Rock Salt a/k/a Rocker • Theme for Jobim • Wallflower.

**GERRY MULLIGAN CLASSICS
Vol. 43** 00843039
Apple Core • A Ballad • Festive Minor • Five Brothers • Line for Lyons • Nights at the Turntable • North Atlantic Run • Song for Strayhorn • Sun on the Stairs • Walkin' Shoes.

KEYBOARD *signature licks*®

These exceptional book/CD packs teach keyboardists the techniques and styles used by popular artists from yesterday and today. Each folio breaks down the trademark riffs and licks used by these great performers.

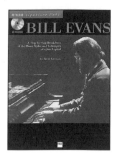

BEST OF BEBOP PIANO
by Gene Rizzo

16 bebop piano transcriptions: April in Paris • Between the Devil and the Deep Blue Sea • I Don't Stand a Ghost of a Chance • If I Were a Bell • Lullaby of Birdland • On a Clear Day (You Can See Forever) • Satin Doll • Thou Swell • and more.
00695734..$19.95

CONTEMPORARY CHRISTIAN
by Todd Lowry

Learn the trademark keyboard styles and techniques of today's top contemporary Christian artists. 12 songs, including: Fool for You (Nichole Nordeman) • The Great Divide (Point of Grace) • His Strength Is Perfect (Steven Curtis Chapman) • How Beautiful (Twila Paris) • If I Stand (Rich Mullins) • Know You in the Now (Michael Card) • and more.
00695753..$19.95

BILL EVANS
by Brent Edstrom

12 songs from pianist Bill Evans, including: Five • One for Helen • The Opener • Peace Piece • Peri's Scope • Quiet Now • Re: Person I Knew • Time Remembered • Turn Out the Stars • Very Early • Waltz for Debby • 34 Skidoo.
00695714..$22.95

BEN FOLDS FIVE
by Todd Lowry

16 songs from four Ben Folds Five albums: Alice Childress • Battle of Who Could Care Less • Boxing • Brick • Don't Change Your Plans • Evaporated • Kate • The Last Polka • Lullabye • Magic • Narcolepsy • Philosophy • Song for the Dumped • Underground.
00695578..$22.95

BILLY JOEL CLASSICS: 1974-1980
by Robbie Gennet

15 popular hits from the '70s by Billy Joel: Big Shot • Captain Jack • Don't Ask Me Why • The Entertainer • Honesty • Just the Way You Are • Movin' Out (Anthony's Song) • My Life • New York State of Mind • Piano Man • Root Beer Rag • Say Goodbye to Hollywood • Scenes from an Italian Restaurant • She's Always a Woman • The Stranger.
00695581..$22.95

BILLY JOEL HITS: 1981-1993
by Todd Lowry

15 more hits from Billy Joel in the '80s and '90s: All About Soul • Allentown • And So It Goes • Baby Grand • I Go to Extremes • Leningrad • Lullabye (Goodnight, My Angel) • Modern Woman • Pressure • The River of Dreams • She's Got a Way • Tell Her About It • This Is the Time • Uptown Girl • You're Only Human (Second Wind).
00695582..$22.95

ELTON JOHN CLASSIC HITS
by Todd Lowry

10 of Elton's best are presented in this book/CD pack: Blue Eyes • Chloe • Don't Go Breaking My Heart • Don't Let the Sun Go Down on Me • Ego • I Guess That's Why They Call It the Blues • Little Jeannie • Sad Songs (Say So Much) • Someone Saved My Life Tonight • Sorry Seems to Be the Hardest Word.
00695688..$22.95

LENNON & MCCARTNEY HITS
by Todd Lowry

Features 15 hits from A-L for keyboard by the legendary songwriting team of John Lennon and Paul McCartney. Songs include: All You Need Is Love • Back in the U.S.S.R. • The Ballad of John and Yoko • Because • Birthday • Come Together • A Day in the Life • Don't Let Me Down • Drive My Car • Get Back • Good Day Sunshine • Hello, Goodbye • Hey Jude • In My Life • Lady Madonna.
00695650..$22.95

LENNON & MCCARTNEY FAVORITES
by Todd Lowry

16 more hits (L-Z) from The Beatles: Let It Be • The Long and Winding Road • Lucy in the Sky with Diamonds • Martha My Dear • Ob-La-Di, Ob-La-Da • Oh! Darling • Penny Lane • Revolution 9 • Rocky Raccoon • She's a Woman • Strawberry Fields Forever • We Can Work It Out • With a Little Help from My Friends • The Word • You're Going to Lose That Girl • Your Mother Should Know.
00695651..$22.95

BEST OF ROCK
by Todd Lowry

12 songs are analyzed: Bloody Well Right (Supertramp) • Cold as Ice (Foreigner) • Don't Do Me Like That (Tom Petty & The Heartbreakers) • Don't Let the Sun Go Down on Me (Elton John) • I'd Do Anything for Love (Meat Loaf) • Killer Queen (Queen) • Lady Madonna (The Beatles) • Light My Fire (The Doors) • Piano Man (Billy Joel) • Point of No Return (Kansas) • Separate Ways (Journey) • Werewolves of London (Warren Zevon).
00695751..$19.95

BEST OF ROCK 'N' ROLL PIANO
by David Bennett Cohen

12 of the best hits for piano are presented in this pack. Songs include: At the Hop • Blueberry Hill • Brown-Eyed Handsome Man • Charlie Brown • Great Balls of Fire • Jailhouse Rock • Lucille • Rock and Roll Is Here to Stay • Runaway • Tutti Frutti • Yakety Yak • You Never Can Tell.
00695627..$19.95

BEST OF STEVIE WONDER
by Todd Lowry

This book/CD pack includes musical examples, lessons, biographical notes, and more for 14 of Stevie Wonder's best songs. Features: I Just Called to Say I Love You • My Cherie Amour • Part Time Lover • Sir Duke • Superstition • You Are the Sunshine of My Life • and more.
00695605..$22.95

Prices, contents and availability subject to change without notice.

FOR MORE INFORMATION, SEE YOUR LOCAL MUSIC DEALER,
OR WRITE TO:

HAL•LEONARD® CORPORATION
7777 W. BLUEMOUND RD. P.O. BOX 13819 MILWAUKEE, WI 53213

Visit Hal Leonard Online at
www.halleonard.com

0304